MODERN MIRACULOUS CURES

MODERN MIRACULOUS CURES

A DOCUMENTED ACCOUNT
OF MIRACLES AND MEDICINE
IN THE 20th CENTURY

BY

Dr François Leuret

formerly President of the Medical Bureau and Bureau of
Scientific Studies of Lourdes

AND

Dr Henri Bon

Translated from the French by
JOHN C. BARRY, DCL
St Andrew's Seminary, Scotland
AND
A. T. MACQUEEN, MB, MRCPE
St Andrew's University, Scotland

London : Peter Davies

NIHIL OBSTAT

John A. Goodwine, J.C.D.
Censor Librorum

IMPRIMATUR

✠ Francis Cardinal Spellman
Archbishop of New York

The *nihil obstat* and *imprimatur* are official declarations
that a book or pamphlet is free of doctrinal or moral error.
No implication is contained therein that those who have
granted the *nihil obstat* and *imprimatur* agree with the
contents, opinions or statements expressed.

FIRST PUBLISHED 1957

Printed in Great Britain for Peter Davies Ltd.
by The Leagrave Press Ltd., Luton and London

LETTER OF APPRECIATION FROM HIS HOLINESS POPE PIUS XII

I have no need to tell you how much the subject with which you are concerned in this volume interests the Holy Father. He has himself more than once had occasion to say, in his discourses and messages, what the Church expects men of science worthy of the name to do in defence of the Faith. He could not but extend the warmest welcome to a work in which a number of cases of miraculous intervention, whereby God has deigned in recent times to manifest His power and goodness to men, are examined with all the most up-to-date technical methods and in a spirit of true scientific loyalty.

J. B. Montini, Subst.

DECLARATION

In conformity with the decrees of the Sovereign Pontiffs and particularly of Pope Urban VIII, the authors declare that their opinions regarding facts or persons other than those whose miraculous character or sanctity has been proclaimed by the Church, do not in any way anticipate the decision of the Holy See. They submit themselves entirely to the judgment of the Holy See, together with every interpretation or theory contained in their work.

Since this work is a study, often covering ground little or never explored before, the opinions expressed in it are the authors' own, and are often no more than hypothetical or tentative in character.

CONTENTS

TRANSLATORS' INTRODUCTION

We should like to draw attention to the following points:

I. Many statements will be found in this book of a dogmatic nature—i.e. pertaining to Catholic dogma, in the strict, rather than the popular sense. Catholics accept these because they believe that Christ our Lord gave infallible teaching authority to St Peter and that that authority rests today with the ruling Pope. It is important to appreciate, however, that the same Church teaches that one should approach her by one's God-given reason, i.e. one should submit her claims to be Christ's properly authorised representative on earth to the ordinary rules for assessing evidence. This approach should be humble and must be accompanied by a sincere desire to know the truth. Catholics believe that any statements made by the Church, and related to faith or morals, are true because they have convinced themselves by reason (among other things) that the Church has the right to teach these truths. The point of this note is that anyone inclined to regard statements of dogma, or of natural theology for that matter, as "mystical," "mumbo-jumbo" or "meaningless," should not do so without first reading up the questions discussed above in some competent textbook or popular exposition of the subjects.

We would earnestly suggest that the activities and beliefs of a society such as the Catholic Church should not be dismissed in summary terms. Many of the most intelligent men in the history of Europe have belonged to it; and the Church, with her long experience of the human pageant, has her reasons for most things. These should be given a careful hearing (or reading) by the genuinely interested individual.

II. The medical translator would like to draw attention to the need for expansion of the medical and research facilities at Lourdes. There is a need for money to allow for the establishment of an all-year-round staff of medical scientists, to observe and record the enormous stream of clinical material passing through it, to examine, to photograph. There is need for research scholarships enabling students of any religious belief to work at and from Lourdes for two or three years.

To illustrate this point let us assume money was available for such appointments. A cure appears to have taken place at Lourdes. The research assistant takes a full history. He is told the diagnosis of malignant disease was established at X Hospital (e.g. Mme Rose Martin, p. 149). Records exist at Y Hospital. The research assistant is able to go to these places, to get photographic copies of the relevant documents and microphotographs of the histological specimens. He talks to pathologists, surgeons, physicians and nurses connected with the case. He interviews all the relevant witnesses and tries to assess their reliability. He sees the patient in a year's time and again in another year. The full report of all this is published in *The Archives of the Lourdes Medical Bureau*—a document bearing comparison in appearance and typographical set-up with *Medical Clinics of North America* or the *British Medical Bulletin*.

At Lourdes, the research assistants, under the guidance of a well-qualified senior staff, and with full secretarial and nursing assistance, with facilities for rapidly finding out what sort of cases have come with the different pilgrimages and further facilities for assembling these quickly, are responsible for giving demonstrations and clinics on any disease.

It is felt that an organisation of the above kind would

make an impact on the scientific world of which Our Lady would approve. It would be evident that at Lourdes the standards of practice and recording were up to that expected by medical scientists all over the world. We hope this book will indicate that, in the prevailing circumstances, they are that already; that this is not widely realised is due to lack of funds necessary to build the necessary buildings, pay the necessary staff and publish and distribute the relevant literature.

III.   It has recently been suggested by the Rev. L. D. Weatherhead in his book, *Psychology, Religion and Healing*,* that the immersion in cold spring water would bring about cures similar to those occurring at Lourdes. We doubt if this matter has ever been statistically analysed. We know of no evidence which shows that the survival rate among moribund and seriously ill animals is increased by immersion in cold spring water. (It seems unlikely that any doctor would permit the experiment on human beings.) The matter should, however, be fairly easily put to the test on animals.

The clergyman indicates that those returning from Lourdes showed disappointment at not being cured. It might be natural to expect some patients to be disappointed, but in general it has not been the experience of those working there—whether medically qualified or not—that patients come back from Lourdes more unhappy than when they went. It would be unlikely that the sick should wish to return so often, and that the numbers should have increased so hugely, if thepsychological effects were generally adverse. In our own experience of not a few pilgrimages the sick find themselves spiritually better and more resigned to their cross, and the majority do not really expect to be cured. In any case, they find the journey a change from routine and the sun does them good. All this may well be attributed to the release of adrenal hormones, but it seems unlikely that as a rule the latter would bring about a feeling of physical well-

* 1951 Hodder & Stoughton, London.

being accompanied by grave psychological depression. The mention of adrenal hormones raises the further question of how far release of these may, associated with suggestion, improve sick pilgrims' health. It seems reasonable, as indicated above, to suppose that such may well be the case. But we have no knowledge of any hormone or drug capable of bringing about cures of the type experienced by Mlle Fretel or Mme Martin. In the case of both, the complete absence of convalescence is quite outside the usual course of events in any serious disease, as is the quite sudden recovery.

In general, cases cited as resembling miraculous cures at Lourdes do not survive close comparison.

Our translation of certain sections of the book has been very free. We have simply summarised anecdotes that sound well in French but do not translate into English happily. Some cases have been left out—e.g. one patient whose case appeared in the French edition objected to being in print. Other cases have been added. We have endeavoured always to convey the meaning of the original without substantial alteration.

We would point out to the reader that some cases carry more conviction than others, e.g. because they are fully reported by medically qualified witnesses. The reader should avoid the temptation to dip into the book. It should be read as a whole or not at all.

CHAPTER I

MIRACLES

Miracles in General[1]

BEFORE Time began, He Who is, IS.

He is pure spirit, three Persons in one nature. He is God: Father, Son and Holy Spirit. He was to reveal this mystery to mankind in the course of the ages.

He is all-Wisdom, and that includes all knowledge, all science. He is all-Love, in the harmony of the Three Persons. He is all-Power.

He is all-Goodness. He created things that they should *be*, because being is good. First, He created them spiritual, like Himself. He gave them knowledge and power, and made them capable of love.

In a tragic moment of pride and ingratitude, some of His spiritual creatures, led by Lucifer, cast themselves loose from God.

His thought conceived and created a non-spiritual world, pregnant with its own beauty and its own joy, and to crown it, creatures twofold in nature, part material and part spiritual, to form a bond between the world of matter and the world of pure spirit.

Out of nothingness emerged matter, product of the divine thought, and under the guidance of that same thought its potentialities developed through infinite space and measureless time into a universe of wonders to be discovered, appreciated, used by numberless generations of creatures.

Such was Creation. Such is Man.

Mysteriously, dramatically, Man proved himself unworthy of his destiny. He cut himself off from God because he wished to be His equal. From that moment he has been thrown back upon his own resources, and is only able to conquer the world of matter in the sweat of his brow. His only access to the world of spirit is through prayer and faith. But grace he can receive, either directly or through the Sacraments.

The material body of Man is ruled by his spiritual soul. His spiritual self is in contact with the Supreme Spirit, God. God upholds and directs the evolution of the material world which He has created, and to which Man's body belongs.

From time to time God, either of His own accord, or in answer to Man's prayer, brings about a modification of the apparently predetermined course of nature. Such was the burning bush which attracted Moses' attention because it did not burn away; such was the passage of the Israelites through the Red Sea; such were the three young Hebrews in the furnace; such was our Lord's multiplication of the loaves and fishes, the cure of the man born blind, of the lepers, of the centurion's servant, and of many others. Such was the raising of Lazarus and the Resurrection of Our Lord after His bloodless body, dead upon the cross and pierced by the lance, had been placed in the tomb.

These are *miracles;* examples of a derogation of the visible laws of the universe: of an exceptional—but by no means surprising—intervention of God in the world which only exists because He sustains it. St Augustine summarised it thus: "We say that all miracles are against nature, but they are not. For how can anything that is caused by God's will be against nature, since the nature of every created thing is nothing else than the will of its Creator?" (De Civ. Dei, Bk. XXI, chap. viii, 2.)

The material world seems to be composed of invisible particles, distributed through infinite space and regulated in their movements and relations with each other by forces of energy.[2]

The combination of these particles, protons, neutrons, electrons, forms a *nucleus*, which when surrounded by a definite number of negative electrons according to the type of body constitutes an *atom*. The size of the atom is measured in angstroms, which equal one ten-millionth of a millimeter. The nucleus represents only a billionth part of the atom's volume. The rest is "empty space" in which the electrons circulate. In consequence almost the whole mass of the atom is in its nucleus. It has been estimated that were it possible to collect them, a cubic centimeter of nuclei of hydrogen, the lightest of the elements, would weigh 100 million tons.

However that may be, this extremely rarified matter, by grouping its atoms into molecules, is the basis of the tremendous variety of chemical bodies, which combine under the action of energy in one form or another into the material world as we know it.

Thus, down the ages, we have the formation of the nebulae, of the stars, the condensation of the earth, the free interplay of physico-chemical forces combining, transforming and moulding the original elements. Then came *Life*, that mysterious principle dominating the physico-chemical forces of nature and guiding them into definite channels so as to ensure the continuity of the species despite the most varied vicissitudes. Finally the scene was set for Man, whose thought harnesses the laws of matter and makes them his servants. And Man's thought rules his body, makes it move and by it bends matter to his will. And Man's thought, face to face with the dynamic richness of matter, the transcendency of Life and his own existence and powers, soars higher yet, and knows God, the supreme fountain-head of all things and of all being.

Occasionally things happen which clash with the well-known laws and processes of creation, and they are closely connected with certain relations of Man to God. The occurrences are known as miracles. "In fact," writes

Alexis Carrel, "everything happens as though God were listening to Man and answering him."[3]

Now science teaches that we can examine any given phenomenon at different levels. A mixture of white flour and black soot appears to us as a grey powder. To a microbe it would not look grey at all, but like a series of black rocks and white rocks. At the subatomic level it would merely be a matter of electrons with slightly different movements.

As Olmer points out: "It is the level of observation which determines the phenomenon, and it is the phenomenon which determines the law deduced by the physicist. Hence we must not be surprised if in two spheres as different as the human and the atomic, the laws do not coincide. The one thing we must be careful to avoid is the desire to anthropomorphize, to bring down to the level of our senses and our understanding, facts which belong to another dimension altogether."[4]

Olmer's rule must be kept in mind when we consider God's intervention in the world He has created. At God's level, our standards have no validity; the laws of matter have no longer any necessity—they are nothing but manifestations of the divine activity, entirely dependent on their Author's will. Our activity in the world can only be exercised through our bodies and through material things in accordance with the laws to which our bodies and matter itself are subject, and then only within the limits prescribed by those laws. The Supreme Being, however, by whom all things exist and are kept in being, is of course unrestricted in His activity. Our criteria of greatness and smallness, of importance and insignificance, are of no value at God's level: the prayer of a child has the same value as that of Plato, the raising of Lazarus is no more difficult than the healing of Malchus' ear.

Nevertheless Man is no stranger to God. His body is of divine creation. So is his soul—and moreover it is spiritual

and mirrors the divine nature. Man in a word occupies a
definite place in the divine plan. It is therefore in no way
extraordinary that there should be contact between Man
and God, and that Man's needs and desires should be the
object of God's loving care, and that where necessary the
course of nature should be diverted to carry out a particular design of the divine will.

Miracles are only marvels at Man's level. At God's
level they are ordinary reasonable actions.

This is precisely the idea developed by St Augustine
in his third book on the Trinity. "Augustine," says his
biographer,[5] "has a wonderful power of appreciating
miracles. He presents miraculous events as the products
of a will working effortlessly and serenely, without waste
of energy. Every year water falls on the earth in its season,
but if the divine power which upholds every creature
suddenly gathers the clouds together after a long and
disastrous drought and contrary to all expectations makes
them fall in rain at the prayer of Elias, we call that a
miracle. God it is who sends thunder and lightning—but
they were miraculous over Mount Sinai because they
were produced in an extraordinary manner. Man plants
and waters, but God gives the increase—grape and vine
and wine are God's handiwork—but the water changed
into wine by Our Lord's word was a miracle even to the
dullest of men. God it is who clothes the trees with green
leaf and blossom, but when Aaron's rod suddenly burst
into flower, there was Divinity in touch with doubting
Humanity. He who raises the dead gives life in the
mother's womb, and bodies are born, grow old and die.
All these things are called natural when they flow past
on the stream of time; they are called marvellous when
they occur in a new way, striking a note of warning or
conveying a message to men. In fact, it is ever one and
the same law at work, but with variations. There is
therefore a great lack of sense in the philosophers' revolt
against the very idea of a miracle."

According to Cardinal Lépicier, we may briefly summarize the requirements for a miracle as follows:

The event must take place comparatively rarely. God did not create the world to interfere constantly with its laws.

Since it is divine in origin, the event must be of a reasonable and moral nature, with no trace of the fantastic or suspicion of sleight of hand.[6]

It must always have a recognisable spiritual purpose.

It must bring about a general or individual good.

It is often instantaneous, but it can be progressive (i.e. where God uses secondary causes).

Before giving her approval the Church normally insists that its effects should be lasting, but that is not absolutely indispensable. Miracles are of their nature limited in time. A cure may be granted to demonstrate the existence of God or the efficacy of prayer, or to permit some useful action to be performed; its purpose once achieved, the disease, arrested as though by an antibiotic, may resume its natural course.

Miracles, in general, correspond to prayer.

The extraordinary intervention of God is to be met with in particular cases and at fairly infrequent intervals right down to our own time, first under Judaism and then under Catholicism, and constitutes one of the proofs of their conformity with the divine plan.

But the sheep that have strayed still belong to the supreme Shepherd. The confusion of tongues at the Tower of Babel, the annihilation of Sodom and Gomorrha, Pharaoh's dreams and the plagues of Egypt, the writing on the wall, "Mané, Thecel, Phares," together with a number of other miracles, were all addressed to unbelievers.

The cure of Naaman the Syrian of leprosy, and Jonas' adventures when he was sent to preach penance to the Ninevites, show that God's Providence is extended to all men and not to the people of Israel alone.[7]

God in His goodness is always ready to hear and answer fervent prayer. As Cardinal Lépicier writes: "We readily admit that miracles can be worked outside the Catholic body in exceptional and individual cases, since the Holy Spirit is free to seek His instruments where He will. This creates no difficulty especially when the miracle-worker is a man of holy life and has no other aim in his works but the honour of God."[8]

The same author concludes that such miracles outside the Catholic Church may have "as their purpose to furnish extra proofs of the existence of the supernatural order."

In any event it is certain that in no religion do miracles occur commonly and with any regularity in our own days, under the full glare of modern scientific investigation, except in the Catholic Church.

Miracles and prodigies must be kept quite distinct. The word "miracle" refers to an event produced by God Himself in infringement of the laws of nature.

But this does not mean that similar events are not produced (with God's permission, of course) by spiritual beings other than God. Thus the Egyptian magicians changed their staffs into serpents, turned the water of the Nile into blood, and caused the frogs to swarm as Aaron and Moses had done at God's behest.[9]

In the Gospel Our Lord foretold: "There will be false Christs and false prophets, who will rise up and shew great signs and wonders, so that if it were possible, even the elect would be deceived."[10] To such as these we may apply the term "prodigy."

That is why, although the witnesses may presume an event to be miraculous, although scientists may examine it in the light of their scientific data and finally conclude that it probably is a miracle, although the theologians may compare these findings with the theological import of the incident and consequently decide upon its supernatural character, it is for the Church alone to pass a definite judgment on the matter. The same holds good for prodigies.

TYPES OF MIRACLES

Miracles, which are exceptions willed by God in the natural course of things, can take on the most varied forms. A few examples will illustrate this:

MATERIAL MIRACLES

The Bible gives an account, among others, of two *astronomical* or *optical* miracles.

At the battle of Gabaon (thirteenth century B.C.) at Josue's prayer "the sun stood in mid-heaven, and for a whole day long did not haste to its setting."[11] We are here told what *appeared*, because in fact the sun does not go round the earth; the earth rotates on its own axis. Therefore the Bible narrative gives scope for various attempts to interpret the phenomenon. Since an interruption of the earth's rotation seems out of proportion with Josue's request—the lengthening of the daylight in that particular locality—and in addition presupposes considerable astronomical complications, Jean Bosler[12] conjectures that after a providential fall of aerolites mentioned in the Bible—"the Lord cast down upon them (i.e. the Amorrhites pursued by Josue's forces) great stones from heaven as far as Azeca. And many . . . were killed . . ."[13]—a "light night" ensued, prolonging the daylight, as has happened before when aerolites have fallen, notably after the fall of June 30th, 1908, in Siberia, which devastated a forest over a radius of fifteen miles. We may also suppose that, by divine intervention, refraction or reflection of the sun's rays was produced in the upper strata of the atmosphere so that the light and appearance of the sun was still visible from the battlefield.

The second miracle shows that scepticism is not a

modern monopoly. In 714 B.C. the king of Juda lay dying.
The prophet Isaias informed him that God had heard his
prayers, that he would recover in three days and would
live for fifteen years more. But King Ezechias was incredulous: "When Ezechias asked what sign should be
given him that his health would be restored, and that he
would set foot in the Lord's temple within three days,
Isaias told him, 'Here is thy proof that the Lord will keep
His promise. Wouldst thou have the shadow on the sun-
dial climb forward by ten hours, or travel backwards as
much?' 'Why' said he, 'it were no great matter that it
should advance ten hours; rather, by my way of it, let it
travel ten hours backwards.' So the prophet Isaias made
appeal to the Lord, and the shadow retraced the last ten
hours it had advanced on the sun-dial of Achaz."[14]

Here again the local and personal character of the
incident invites an optical interpretation based on the
refraction or reflection of the light.

To miracles such as these may be compared Pope St
Pius V's vision of the naval victory of Lepanto from his
window in the Vatican in 1571.[15] In this case something
like a mirage could have been miraculously produced in
the sky.[16]

Finally, in modern times, on October 13th, 1917, at
the end of the sixth and last apparition at Fatima, thousands of onlookers, not merely at the place of the apparitions itself but also some distance (as much as thirty miles)
away, saw the sun, silver-white, whirl round three times
like a wheel of fire, throwing off opalescent shafts of light,
and then appear to zigzag down toward the earth, and
finally return to its original place and to its ordinary
appearance. The phenomenon lasted altogether about
ten minutes. The bishop of Leiria, Mgr José da Silva,
observes that it "was watched by crowds of people of all
types and every social class, by believers as well as unbelievers, by reporters representing the chief Portuguese
newspapers, and even by people several miles away,

thereby destroying any theory of collective illusion." He adds that the event was not recorded by any observatory.[17]

We may therefore assume that the "great miracle" which during the apparition of July 13th the children were warned to expect in October involved either the sun's rays over the Fatima district or the atmospheric strata through which they passed.

Other "physical" miracles are described in the Israelites' crossing of the Red Sea during the Exodus, and of the Jordan when they were about to enter the Promised Land.

The first is told as follows: "Meanwhile, Moses stretched out his hand over the sea, and the Lord cleared it away from their path. All night a fierce sirocco blew, and the Lord turned the sea into dry land, the waters parting this way and that. So the Israelites went through the midst of the sea dry-shod, with its waters towering up like a wall to right and left."[18]

The second runs thus: "So the people left their encampment to go across Jordan, the priests who carried the ark marching at their head. And when these began wading out, as soon as their feet were under water (it was harvest-time, and the Jordan had risen to the full height of its banks), the stream above them halted in its course. Far up, all the way from the city of Adom to the place called Sarthan, these upper waters looked like a swelling mound; and the waters below flowed on into the Desert Sea, that is now called the Dead Sea, till they disappeared altogether. And so the people marched on to the assault of Jericho . . ."[19]

The miracle is presented in two forms: at the Red Sea, the parting of the water was due to a strong wind driving it back so that it stood like two walls on either side. At the Jordan, a dam of water was created upstream, and the water downstream flowed away, leaving the river bed dry. Almighty God harnesses natural forces to His purpose and limits His direct intervention to the barest minimum.

Other miracles are concerned with the nature of particular substances. Thus the first plague of Egypt involved the changing of water into blood: ". . . the river turned into blood. All the fishes in the river died, and its waters stank, so that the Egyptians could not drink river water any longer, and there was blood all over the land of Egypt."[20]

At the marriage feast of Cana, when His mother remarked that there was no wine, Jesus had the six water pots filled with water, and when it was drawn out again, it was found to be wine.[21]

We may assume that in these cases the result was produced by intra-atomic or molecular action.

There are also miracles which consist in a multiplication of substance.

The most famous of these are of course the multiplication of the five loaves and two fishes, and of seven loaves and a few fishes by Our Lord when He wished to feed several thousand people. In the first instance twelve baskets of scraps were gathered up, and in the second, seven.

In modern times a number of similar occurrences have been recorded by Oliver Leroy. In 1825, at La Puye, near Poitiers, France, thirty bushels of grain, blessed in June by Father André (St Andrew Hubert Fournet), fed the whole community of the Daughters of the Cross (at times more than two hundred persons) for six months, although that quantity would normally have lasted no more than a week. The two heaps, one of wheat and one of barley, did not diminish.[22]

In 1883, in the same convent, it was the wine barrels which proved inexhaustible after the venerable founder, now dead, had been invoked, and six weeks' ration lasted for three months, despite the fact that during that period a retreat was held, which at one time more than doubled the number of persons in the house. These facts were sworn to by the witnesses at the canonisation process.

Similar occurrences are attributed to the intercession of St Francis Regis at the prayer of the Curé of Ars in 1829, of St Germaine Cousin at the prayer of St Mary Pelletier in 1845, of St Mary Magdalene Postel in 1871, of St John Bosco in 1886 and of others.[23]

To explain the means used in these cases we may have recourse either to a creation of new substance, or to an addition to or multiplication of existing substance. An act of creation does not seem necessary; we know that God does not work unnecessary miracles. Further, the hypothesis of an addition does not seem probable if we bear in mind that Our Lord did not just produce the wine at the marriage feast of Cana, but used the water with which the jars had been filled at His command, and if we recall that His first step in the desert was to ask what food was available, and that it was *that* food which was made so superabundant, without the appearance of any other. The same is true of modern miracles: the existing food seems to have a sort of crystallising effect on extraneous atomic or molecular elements, perhaps borrowed directly from the atmosphere.[24]

The truth is that we are faced with phenomena which are out of proportion with the normal mechanics of nature. But we are by no means in the realm of fairy stories. As Christ Himself insists, the starting point is material; there is a rapid, ultra-rapid, even instantaneous production of finite objects, but the basic elements which nature uses in the normal way to produce such objects are present in the atmosphere, and nature derives them from it. Are the chemical and biological processes known to us the only possible ones? Is time an absolute value? Miracle there is, to be sure, for nature does nothing like it, and God is there: but the phenomenon is not at complete variance with our scientific knowledge.

MIRACLES IN LIVING THINGS
The plagues of Egypt include several examples: the

multiplication of the frogs, flies, beetles and locusts, as well as the cattle plague.

It is worth noticing that in the case of the locusts God used a material instrument, an east wind which blew all day and all night, carrying the locusts with it. The plague came to an end because the same thing happened: a strong west wind arose and blew them into the Red Sea.[25]

As for the cattle plague, its miraculous character consists in the fact that it descended on the Egyptians' cattle in one night while those of the Israelites remained unharmed.

When Jacob asked Laban to give him as his wages all the parti-coloured animals born in a flock of sheep and goats confided to his care, all of them of one colour, he hit upon the plan of putting sticks partly stripped of their bark, and therefore striped or spotted, into the drinking troughs. As a result the lambs and kids born of the flock were spotted or speckled, while the sickly beasts, which did not undergo this treatment—for Jacob only wanted the best—gave birth to lambs and kids of one colour.[26] The ruse may make us smile, in spite of its evident success, for it required divine intervention. But God nevertheless used a material instrument, apparently ineffectual of itself, which in this particular case was made to have a miraculous biological influence.

MIRACLES IN THE HUMAN BODY

Most of Our Lord's miracles belong to this category. We need not delay here, because the modern miraculous cures to be reviewed later will give us ample opportunity to note the wide variety of their characteristics.

But what we have already said about the presence of natural agents, utilised and activated by God, even in the most famous miracles, ought to warn us that these characteristics can be extremely varied, and that we must not be so simple as to expect a regular and featureless transition from sickness to cure, and that it can sometimes be a very delicate matter to distinguish between the normal process of recovery and the natural factors used and activated by God to produce a cure.

INTELLECTUAL AND SPIRITUAL MIRACLES

Miracles, the direct and extraordinary intervention of God in the normal course of nature, are not confined to the realm of matter. We have seen that God created the spiritual world and that man possesses the double nature of a spiritual as well as a material being. If man's body can be the object of a supernatural intervention on God's part, so can his soul. St Thomas, writing of St Paul's conversion, puts it thus: "The common and normal process of justification, whereby God moves the soul of man interiorly to be converted to Himself, first by an imperfect conversion leading gradually to perfect conversion, is not a miracle. But when God moves the soul so powerfully that it instantly attains to a certain perfection of grace, as was the case with St Paul, using at the same time an external prodigy such as his miraculous fall [from his horse], then this conversion is a miracle. That is why the conversion of St Paul is solemnly commemorated by the Church as miraculous."[27]

On the other hand, even when there is an absence of outward material signs such as those which accompanied St Paul's conversion, no conversion is purely spiritual in character. During his lifetime man's soul and body are one whole. By following the development of his ideas a psychologist can trace the course of a normal conversion, the particular incidents which quickened its tempo, the working of the mind, the gradual process of conviction cemented by the grace of God. A psychiatrist can recognise a false conversion based on hallucination or emotion. A theologian can judge the reality and depth of conversion.

This means that psychological, psychiatric and theological tests can be applied to determine the normal or extraordinary character of a conversion, just as material tests can help to determine the normal or abnormal character of a physical cure.

There is, then, every reason to speak of "spiritual miracles" as ecclesiastical writers not infrequently do, and to attach great importance to them in the theological and philosophical fields.

Mgr Charue, bishop of Namur, in his inaugural sermon for the "Année Sociale" on December 8th, 1948, relates an incident of this kind: "In a Belgian village church, during the war, a mother knelt in tears before the statue of Our Lady. Her son had just been arrested by the Germans, and his life was in the greatest danger. Unfortunately he had lost his faith and had devoted himself, body and soul, to the most pernicious and anti-Christian doctrines. The poor woman prayed thus: 'I've never been able to do anything with him. I don't ask you, my Mother, to bring him back to me safe and sound, but at least don't let him die unrepentant. I'm handing all my rights as his mother over to you; do what you like with him.' As it happened, the prodigal son remembered the Blessed Virgin in his prison cell, and promised to change his way of living if he were set free. He meant to use every means, even those in which he did not believe! He was set free, but forgot his promise. Later he was imprisoned again, and once more set at liberty. But he only intensified his subversive activities, faithless and lawless. There seemed no hope that his mother's prayers would ever be answered.

"Suddenly, in September 1945, our friend was tormented with the idea of going to Beauraing. He kept putting it away, but each time it returned, stronger than ever, until it began to haunt him day and night. Finally he yielded, and set off for Beauraing on the last Sunday of the month, arriving at ten o'clock in the morning. He asked for the site of the Apparitions, knowing nothing of their history, in fact believing neither in God nor devil.

He stood there at the entrance to the enclosure, facing the hawthorn, without a prayer, wondering why he was there at all, when suddenly he was struck down. As he tells us, 'I tried to save myself from falling, but in vain, and I clung to the back of the last bench. For quite a time I saw nothing but the statue of Our Lady of the Hawthorn. I felt as though everything in me had turned upside down, and I wept over my past life; but I wept for joy too, for I was conscious that something new had come into my soul.' "[28]

On December 14th, 1926, Fr Leseur, O.P., a former pupil of Landouzy,[29] told the story of his conversion to a regional meeting of the French Medical Society of St Luke. It happened in 1914, and he passed from absolute unbelief to full faith under the influence of an irresistible psychological impulse. Incidents of this type are fairly common and their supernatural character is unmistakable.

MIRACLES OF FAITH

Although the various classes of miracle just described afford tangible proofs of God's presence and are a guarantee of the divine mission of the Jewish people and of the Church, there are other miracles which do not fall within the scope of our senses and which every Christian must take on faith, on Christ's word and the Church's teaching. Such is the miracle of the Holy Eucharist.

"Innumerable miracles", writes Pope Leo XIII, "surround the miracle of transubstantiation which is in its way the greatest of all miracles. Here indeed all the laws of nature are suspended; the substance of the bread and wine is completely changed into the body and blood of Jesus Christ. The appearances of bread and wine remain, but stripped of their substance and upheld by the divine power alone. Christ's body is everywhere present at one and the same time wherever the Sacrament is consecrated."[30]

But miracles of faith are in no way contrary to reason,

and we are not obliged to fall back blindly on the ultimate argument that God can do all things. In the first place, when Our Lord instituted this Sacrament He took bread and wine, in which are to be found all the necessary ingredients of the human body. There are therefore no reasonable grounds for denying that the bread and wine could become the body and blood of Our Lord on the altar.

But the appearances of the bread and wine are still there! In this respect one of the findings of modern science may come to our aid. It is the notion of *pseudomorphosis* in mineralogy. We quote from Olmer:[31] "Bisulphide of iron (FeS_2) is to be found in two entirely different forms, *pyrites* which has crystals belonging to the cubic group and *marcasite* which belongs to the orthorhombic group. In textbooks of mineralogy these two dimorphous forms have always been set down side by side, each under its own name. The discovery of X-rays has completely altered this view. In many cases slides made of pyrites powder and of marcasite powder have been found to be absolutely identical. What has happened is this: of the two forms, only pyrites remains stable at normal temperatures. However, in the process of crystallisation different conditions of temperature and pressure combine to produce marcasite crystals. But if the samples are kept for a considerable period of time, they change gradually into pyrites, *but without giving any outward signs of the transformation*—they somehow retain the imprint of the original crystal. This is an example of pseudomorphosis, a phenomenon common enough in mineralogy, where (as elsewhere) clothes do not always make the man!"[32]

Occasionally visible miracles are worked to enable certain souls to believe more easily in miracles of faith. Thus the Holy Eucharist has been the occasion of numerous striking miracles, such as that of Bolsena in 1263, when blood flowed from the Sacred Host held by a priest who was tormented by doubts. It has been shown else-

c

where[33] that the hypothesis of "bacillus prodigiosus" in this case was sheer fancy, since the biological characteristics of the microbe and the conditions in which the incident occurred were utterly incompatible.

This very brief sketch of some of the types of miracles shows that we are far removed from the realm of fairy tales, of magic wands which make enchanted castles appear and disappear or turn men into beasts in the twinkling of an eye, and all the rest of it. We may truly say that the divine intervention sticks to nature. Certainly the phenomena encountered exceed the potentialities of natural agents, but these are made to play a definite if partial role according to their capacities. As Cardinal Lépicier remarks,[34] God does not violate the laws of nature. When He works miracles He harnesses them, suspending those of their effects which do not answer to His purpose and Himself making up for their deficiencies. It follows that the scientific study of miracles gives us a better insight into God's action. At the same time their material element convinces us both of their reality and of the wisdom of the Creator.

The Classification of Miracles

Miracles can be classified in various ways according to one's point of view. That which we have just outlined is to some extent superficial. The theologians adopt methods of classification which go very much deeper. One of the most common is the division into miracles *supra naturam, contra naturam* and *praeter naturam.*

Miracles *supra naturam* (surpassing nature) go beyond the forces of nature altogether: for example, the raising of the dead to life. The soul has left the body, and God alone can bring it back. The reason why it has left the body is because the body is no longer fit to be its dwelling place and instrument or else because God has withdrawn the soul, thereby causing decomposition to set in.[35] A soul which returns to a dead body must receive from God a peculiar power to revitalise the body, or else the body must first be restored by divine Omnipotence so that it can respond to the soul's impulse.

Miracles *contra naturam* (against nature) are those in which the effect produced seems contrary to that which ought to have taken place according to the laws of nature. The classical example is that of the three children of Israel who remained unscathed in the furnace.[36] As far as we can see, God did not give them a sort of incombustibility analogous with the impassibility of the glorified body after the resurrection of the dead;[37] instead, a natural instrument seems to have been used to work the miracle.

The text runs thus: "But an angel of the Lord had gone down into the furnace with Azarias and his companions; and he drove the flames away from it, making a wind blow in the heart of the furnace, like the wind that brings the dew. So that these three were untouched, and the fire brought them neither pain nor discomfort."[38]

The previous verses are worth noting: ". . . the flame rose forty-nine cubits above the furnace itself, breaking out and burning such Chaldæans as stood near it."[39]

It all looks as though when the angel came down into the furnace, he was accompanied by a column of cold air which ensured the safety of the three victims and caused a strong centrifugal draught, sending the flames shooting outward upon the Chaldeans. This use of a natural agent by the angel might reduce this miracle to the third category.[40]

Miracles *praeter naturam* (alongside nature) only exceed the forces of nature relatively and in the manner in which they are brought about. Most miraculous cures belong to this class—the disease may be curable in certain conditions of time, of the physical state of the organism and of therapeutic treatment. The miracle lies in the fact that the cure is wrought by divine intervention without these conditions. We shall return to this point later.

Chapter II

MIRACULOUS CURES

Man's original sin, as well as the actual sins of men, has separated Man from God and made him a prey to sickness and death. "Death was never of God's fashioning; not for His pleasure does life cease to be; what meant His creation, but that all created things should have being? No breed has He created on earth but for its thriving; none carries in itself the seeds of its own destruction. Think not that mortality bears sway on earth . . ."[1]

But Man continues to bring down on his own head the fatal consequences of his infringement of nature's laws. His wars, the barbarism of his concentration camps and gas chambers, his individual crimes undermine, wound, torture and destroy the human frame, and cause the spectres of famine, disease and epidemic to stalk through the world. By his immorality he ruins his health and infects his family and descendants with venereal and other diseases; by his laziness and self-indulgence he poisons his nervous system and blood-stream; by his selfishness he robs his neighbour to enrich himself, leaving him to die of poverty and hunger.

But God has pity on Man; in times past He guided the Patriarchs, gave the Law to Moses, His Son became man to restore mankind to its original destiny, and to reopen the road to salvation.

He has pity on men, and works miracles to open their eyes to the truth. In His pity He wants to alleviate human misery, so Christ healed the sick. To prove the holiness of His servants, God heals the sick. To guarantee apparitions and visions, God heals the sick.

Finally, He just has pity . . . and, when faced with the suffering, the pain, the faith of an invalid, with the helpless anguish of parents, the threat of moral and material disaster hanging over children, He heals the sick.

The ignorance, weakness and wickedness of men bring down upon them the inevitable and often tragic effects of disregarding nature's laws. The faith, hope and charity of those who have listened to the word of God make their appeal to His goodness. And God's pity grants that the operation of His laws is suspended, or directed toward the cure of the sick.

Characteristics of Miraculous Cures

Before even presuming, let alone stating definitely, that a cure is miraculous, it must be quite certain that the disease really existed.

This seems so obvious that it is hardly worth mentioning. On the contrary, it is of great importance to belabour the point. Every step must be taken to exclude all possibility of faking a cure either for the sake of publicity or of reaping the advantages of being the object of a miracle or of casting ridicule on our religion. As we shall see, such things have happened.

Hence all forms of sham disease caused by auto-suggestion—such as the unconscious reproduction of the symptoms of a coxalgia previously witnessed by the patient; ankylosis or paralysis resulting from an injury either through fear of it or through the shock of seeing it in one similarly injured; or the appearance of symptoms described in some medical book or article which the patient has consulted when feeling unwell—all these must be ruthlessly weeded out.

The diagnosis must have been accurate. A layman can undoubtedly observe certain symptoms and describe certain injuries correctly, but his tendency will often be to use exaggerated terminology—to describe diarrhœa as dysentery, a slight haemorrhage as "pints of blood," a slight cyanosis as "black in the face," lack of appetite as starvation and so on.

Thus as a general rule any diagnosis not made by a doctor is open to suspicion.

Even a doctor's diagnosis cannot always be accepted without a grain of salt. It often happens that a doctor is obliged to treat his patient according to the symptoms without being able to determine the nature of the disease with any certainty, and in such cases he will not hesitate to give the family an approximate diagnosis which he knows is largely guesswork. It is therefore imperative to have an exact diagnosis, guaranteed as such by the doctor, and supported as far as possible by objective proofs—a careful description of the symptoms, laboratory tests, X-ray plates and the like. The patient's family circle may then be able to supplement these with interesting corroborative details.

We shall see later that the ecclesiastical authorities are extremely strict, and rightly so, in their insistence on exact diagnosis.

Once the existence of the disease is established, a cure, to be accepted as miraculous, must be in some way abnormal.

Ideally, the disease should be incurable, either by its very nature (e.g. certain cancers, some diseases of the blood, certain bone disorders or lesions of the nervous system), or because though relatively cureable, it has reached a stage where recovery is out of the question and death inevitable.

Although our knowledge in this latter field is still somewhat limited, it is likely that the progress made in pathology will steadily increase it, so that we shall be able to make better forecasts than those based merely on our "clinical sense." It will then be possible to pin-point the miraculous element in cures of diseases curable in themselves, which patient and doctor may only presume today, without being able to prove anything definite.

The miraculous nature of a cure may be admitted in the case of a curable disease, not merely when it has gone too far, as we have just pointed out, but also:

If it could only have been cured by medical or surgical treatment, such as X-rays, radium, amputation, the use of serums, transfusion, which however were not used:

If the cure was obtained in such a short space of time that the normal processes of recovery could not have taken place—as in the instantaneous closing of a wound, the instantaneous or ultra-rapid healing of a fair-sized tubercular lesion, etc. The time factor is clearly of the first importance in the study of miraculous cures.[2]

Miraculous cures may present special characteristics:

General disturbance: Dr Le Bec, following Dr Duret, notes that sometimes "the sick person experiences a sensation of agony, exhaustion or intense cold. At times they shiver and tremble, or even fall into a syncope and seem on the point of death; they go pale with a corpse-like pallor. Then suddenly all this is replaced by a feeling of calm, peace and well-being. The sick person feels within himself that he is cured."

Local pain: In some cases intense local pain is felt, usually for a very short time. Dr Le Bec suggests that this pain, this sudden discomfort, is closely connected with the instantaneous nature of the cure. These symptoms may be compared with similar states at the crisis of certain diseases and in the effects of shock, whether spontaneous or not. They indicate an organic disturbance, but their short duration and rapid disappearance cannot be reconciled with the normal course of the disease or lesion. In fact many instantaneous cures are quite free from them. But when they are present they seem to imply God's use of normal or "activated" physiological processes.

Absence of the physiological phenomena which normally accompany an immediate cure: disappearance of œdema without polyuria, reabsorption of large tumours with no signs of uræmic symptoms and without increase in temperature as a result of disintegration, etc.[3]

Complete absence of convalescence: One remarkable consequence of miraculous cures is generally the complete absence of convalescence, the body returning at once to full functional activity, whether local or general. People suffering from cancer, gastric ulcers or tubercular enteritis begin to eat normal quantities of every kind of food; people unable to move for months and years because of old fractures walk for several miles; people with lung or heart trouble climb stairs or hills with ease.

For an extraordinary cure to be accepted as miraculous, it must take place in connection with an act of worship, either on the part of the sick person (a prayer or a pilgrimage), or of others (prayers, a blessing, use of relics and the like).

We must not however exclude the possibility of God in His goodness and wisdom working a cure without having been asked, for reasons of His own. Nor may we overlook the fact that God may, in His mysterious providence, permit other spiritual beings to play a part in healing disease. But we are primarily concerned with cures worked by God, miraculous cures, and the religious element is therefore of the first importance.

Finally, the Church demands that there should be no relapse over a long period of time, usually at least a year, before setting the seal of her approbation on a miraculous cure.

But it is evident that the complete disappearance of a tumour, the sudden filling up of pulmonary cavities, the instantaneous healing of a wound cannot be taken as natural even if the tumour reappears or tuberculosis recurs or the wound reopens several weeks or months afterward.

The Church may refuse to register a cure as miraculous but that does not prevent it from being taken as such from a scientific point of view.

ATTITUDE OF THE CHURCH AND SCIENCE

It is worth emphasising that the Church and science

do not look at alleged miraculous cures from precisely the same angle.

The Church received her doctrine and her mission from divine revelation and in particular from the teaching of Our Lord. Striking miracles, reported in the Bible, provided proofs of that revelation and of Christ's divine nature, as He Himself pointed out.

Subsequent miracles may be God's way of guaranteeing His less tangible favours—apparitions, visions, holiness. In the case of such miraculous proofs the Church owes it to herself to insist upon absolute certainty.

Other miracles take place in public, as a pledge of God's presence and assistance. It is essential to make sure that such phenomena are not faked by deceit or illusion, for that would cause confusion and throw suspicion on genuine miracles. The Church alone has the right to decide upon the supernatural character of a phenomenon; while taking into account the findings of human science, she and she alone possesses the light of the Holy Spirit and jurisdiction in the things of God. Here again the Church must be extremely strict in her judgments.

There are other miracles which are more or less private in character. With regard to them, it is for experts and individuals to form their own opinion with the help of theologians, who, without in any way prejudicing the decision of the Church, may give reasonable weight to probabilities. But these are never more than personal opinions—this applies to theologians as well as to others —and they can only be accepted as long as the Church does not declare otherwise.

Clearly medical men have an essential part to play where both public and private miracles are concerned. In point of fact, the Church neither seeks nor advertises miracles. On the contrary she waits until the public, the witnesses particularly, bring alleged miraculous happenings before her and submit them to her judgment. That being so, it is obvious that the doctor is the man best qualified to declare whether a cure shows evidence of overstepping the natural order or not.

It would be wrong to say that this is not part of the doctor's job. His job is not merely to treat people—he has a human duty to perform with regard to his patients and their families. In all but exceptional circumstances he is bound to tell them the truth. He has no right to take the credit himself for a cure which he knows was not due to his treatment. It would be disloyal for him to credit nature with a cure which seems to exceed the powers of nature when the patient and those looking after him take another explanation for granted, whether he agrees with it or not. He must say what he knows; it is for others to draw their own conclusions if he feels that he cannot do so himself.

On the other hand, if he himself believes in the miracle, it would be very shabby of him to decline the role of "God's witness" offered him by providence.

However that may be, it is evident that the Church must leave no loophole when she admits the miraculous character of a cure. She cannot involve her children in error nor compromise her own authority and mission by imprudence. She must prove conclusively that God alone could have been the author of the event under consideration.

Those miraculous cures which do receive her approbation are in reality types, pointers, samples of what we may reasonably expect and recognise in everyday experience.

Science, for its part, although the methods and procedure are much the same, can afford to be much more liberal. It has no need to prove that only God could have worked the wonder. It has only to determine whether or not nature could have produced the cure in the circumstances and whether there was any possibility of some external intervention, presumably divine. It can therefore accept cases on grounds of probability or because of their scientific interest, although absolute proof may be wanting.

Conversely, the Church may use supplementary criteria to establish the miraculous character of a cure in which the purely medical facts do not at first sight carry conviction. Finally, while the Church's primary task is to recognise the hand of God, the gradual unfolding of the physiological phenomena and the biological processes caused by divine intervention can be, for science, a fascinating study in themselves.

MODERN MIRACULOUS CURES

Miraculous cures belonging to modern times have a special interest to the student.

Firstly, the sceptics who do not believe in miracles are inclined to reject miraculous cures worked in times or in places permeated with the atmosphere of faith. They use such expressions as: "In the Middle Ages . . . in an aura of mystery and credulity . . . among peoples saturated with the religious spirit . . . ." and so on.

But modern miracles, especially the cures at Lourdes from the year 1858 onward, have burst upon a world infected with Voltaire's sarcasm and Renan's scepticism, impregnated with atheistic liberalism[4] and blinded by its worship of pseudo-science, and brought it face to face with an extraordinary renascence of the miraculous.

Even unbelievers and atheists have been cured.

Modern miraculous cures have this peculiarity, that modern science enables us to establish their presence far more surely than ever before. The connection between auscultation and pulmonary lesions, discovered by Laënnec and his successors, and the use of radiological techniques enable us to know with certainty the condition of the lungs before and after cure. The discoveries of Pasteur and the bacteriologists enable us to detect pathogenic bacilli in the patient's sputum, urine, blood and pus, and their absence after the cure. Serological methods, skin reaction, agglutination and flocculation tests are all useful. Neurological investigations make it possible to distinguish between organic paralysis and hysterical manifestations, whereas the great canonist, Prospero Lambertini, had to set all paralysis aside as suspect. Deafness and hearing troubles can now be established conclusively. In the same way ophthalmoscopy enables us to check an alleged case of blindness by accurate observation, particularly of the retina, optic nerve and increase of intracranial pressure. True, the public often applies the word "miracle" to facts in regard of which science could not declare itself satisfied, but there exists a whole host of miraculous cures which do comply with the most stringent requirements of science.

The cures worked in bygone times focused attention principally upon their divine origin, but modern miraculous cures are studied by scientists for their own sake, for example by Mangin[5] and Alexis Carrel, who came back many times to Lourdes in search of the secret of cellular multiplication in cures of wounds and fistulae. In addition, medical theses have been written about them.[6] Modern miraculous cures are therefore a subject for scientific investigation in themselves, quite apart from their supernatural origin.

But as products of divine intervention they create problems which without the present-day development of scientific knowledge could not even be envisaged, let alone satisfactorily explained by hypotheses. We have already met with outstanding examples of the part played by modern scientific discoveries in our analysis of the types of miracle.

Obviously divine Omnipotence is at the root of miraculous cures, but the processes set in motion by that Omnipotence are a subject to which neither theologians nor scholars can remain indifferent.

THE STUDY OF CURES

Unfortunately the study of miraculous cures is fraught with very serious difficulties.

The Church's attitude is, on the whole, one of calm detachment. To be sure, these cures provide a tangible proof of her doctrine of the goodness of God, the power of prayer and of faith, and the possibility of divine interference with the normal course of things, but proofs of this sort have been common enough down the ages, particularly during Our Lord's lifetime, so that new cures are no novelty to her.

She only consents to look into such things when they are submitted to her for judgment regarding their miraculous character in order to furnish evidence of an individual's reputation for sanctity or to establish the reality of spiritual favours.

The question of miraculous cures is, therefore, one primarily affecting the people concerned, who welcome the cure with joy and form their own conclusions about its philosophical and spiritual character. Some quietly enjoy their good fortune, others shout it to the four winds like the leper in the Gospel,[7] others leave a thank-offering at some shrine, but few think of presenting themselves at once to their doctor or parish priest.[8]

For one thing, they do not realise the scientific and apologetic value of such an immediate examination. They are cured, and that is all that matters. They overlook the requirements of science and theology.

For another, it must be admitted that they are not always sure of their reception. And they have every reason to be apprehensive, for doctors are on their guard against humiliating errors of diagnosis and the aberrations of overwrought nerves or psychic disorders, while theologians are reluctant to admit that God has taken liberties with the limits they have very properly assigned to Him.

Doubtless there are many people who rush to acclaim as a miracle what is no more than a natural recovery, a nervous phenomenon or an illusion, but it too often happens that a case is written off as an illusion through preconceived notions and without proper examination.

God's activity may not be discernible on superficial investigation because of His use of secondary causes. It is natural to expect a miracle to leap to the eye. And doctors and theologians are naturally inclined to try to show that there is no miracle, rather than to discover exactly what occurred.

This tendency is well known, and persons who have been "cured" may be content to rejoice in their own small circle rather than risk unpleasant interrogations, incredulous smiles and even, perchance, a rude rebuff. They may also fear that their personal affairs and misfortunes will be brought too much into the limelight.

Apart from that, even where the miracle is of a striking character, there are all sorts of difficulties to be encountered regarding the exact condition of the patient before the cure. The doctors in charge of the case may not agree, various treatments may have been tried and doubt thrown on the precise nature of the disease, the doctors may not have kept their files up to date and may be unable to trust their memories, documents such as temperature charts, analyses, radiographs may have gone astray.

Finally, there are doctors who hold that "miracles don't happen," and refuse to examine the facts, to stand by their previous statements or to hand over documents which might bring to light facts at variance with their convictions. We recall one patient suffering from plastic peritonitis. The main adhesions were removed by operation. There was a relapse, confirmed by X-ray. The surgeon decided to postpone a further operation because the patient was capable of taking liquid nourishment. The sick woman made a pilgrimage to Lourdes and her cure was proved by radiography. But the original radiologist refused to hand over the X-ray reports previous to the cure either to the patient or her doctor, and went so far as to inform us personally that he had never seen the patient before her departure for Lourdes!

Miraculous cures are of their nature rare. The study of rare phenomena demands that everyone should co-operate to the best of his ability. It is clear from what we have said that for one reason or another this is not always the case.

Besides, it is still a difficult matter to undertake the description or discussion of miraculous cures before learned societies, even when these are Catholic, because of human respect, prejudice, fruitless but reiterated arguments on matters of principle, insufficient knowledge of the possible complications of such cases and the like. The same is true of their publication in medical periodicals.[9]

Consequently the best studied of all cures, those used in causes of canonisation, remain buried in ecclesiastical archives, while here and there various types of cures are described in a manner calculated to edify and interest, but hardly scientific. Because the medical profession has insufficient documentation at its disposal it is liable to form erroneous ideas of miraculous cures.

A sincere desire to know the truth ought to dispel most of these difficulties.

Chapter III

MODERN MIRACULOUS CURES
IN OUR EXPERIENCE

In every epoch, in every land and in most religions there have been well-known holy places where cures have been worked, attributed for the most part to the action of God. In this chapter we shall deal first with cures that have taken place at shrines and sanctuaries, secondly with cures connected with miracle-workers, and lastly we shall offer an example of a cure of a private nature.

What we have already said concerning miracles and religions makes it clear that the fact that God answers prayer, by whatever name He may be called, need not surprise us. But it is well to bear in mind, as the history of medicine shows, that in many non-Christian religions the practice of medicine was the prerogative of the priesthood or of certain priestly classes.[1] In these circumstances it is impossible to distinguish the part played by God, by spiritual beings other than God, or by medicine in the cures recorded.

Medicine had its origin in the temples of Aesculapius, and many of our thermal resorts still use the medicinal properties of wells or springs decorated with ancient thanksgiving tablets.

Christian sanctuaries are in a different category altogether. They are exclusively centres of prayer. No regular treatment is given and there are no doctors available for consultation. Moreover many of the cures connected with them take place at a distance, after the sick person has invoked the saint of the sanctuary in his own home. And when there is a spring, chemical analysis of the water shows that it contains nothing of therapeutic value—and anyhow many of the "cures" have been worked without using it at all.

Christian sanctuaries are therefore entirely spiritual in character. The cures worked there are gratuitous manifestations of God's presence and love, a source of encouragement to faith, a reward for the invalid's steadfast trust and for the sacrifices and sufferings undertaken during the pilgrimage.

Some shrines are spoken of as though no cures were ever worked anywhere else. Without doubt they are favoured with numerous or particularly striking cures for a time. But many sanctuaries which in their day were world-famous for their cures, no longer seem to have the "gift." Indeed there is hardly a church or chapel which could not have its own Golden Book of the cures worked in answer to the prayers said there.

There is, then, no essential connection between the healing process and the *place* of the sanctuary. When cures do take place there in great numbers, that is in accordance with God's inscrutable designs, but there is no law about it.

The modern era is dominated by the renown of the cures worked at Lourdes since the apparitions of the Blessed Virgin to Bernadette Soubirous in 1858. Since that time the flow of cures has continued year by year, some extraordinary, some less remarkable, to such an extent that a medical investigation bureau was set up in 1882 by Dr de Saint-Maclou to study and verify them. We shall return to this subject later.

OUR LADY OF FATIMA

One of the most recent sanctuaries is that of Fatima, a Portuguese hamlet where the Blessed Virgin appeared to three little shepherd children on six occasions between May 13th and October 13th, 1917. On October 13th, 1930, after a very careful and detailed inquiry had been held, Mgr. José da Silva, Bishop of Leiria, issued the

D

following decree: "(1) That the visions of the children at the Cova da Iria in the parish of Fatima in this diocese on the thirteenth day of each month between May and October 1917 are deserving of credit: (2) That the cult of Our Lady of Fatima is officially permitted."

Since the time of the Apparitions many people have claimed to have been cured at Fatima or by invoking Our Lady of Fatima. The sick have flocked there on pilgrimage. To accommodate them a hospital has been built near the sanctuary, and a medical investigation bureau was set up, first under the direction of Dr Pereira Gens, assisted by the doctors present (at times as many as thirty). Early in 1950 Dr Meyrelles do Souto of Lisbon was given the task of reorganising the medical services.

The sick are interviewed by the doctors on their arrival in Fatima. Between 1926 and 1937 the medical bureau entered about 15,000 on its registers. The official organ of the sanctuary, the *Voz de Fátima*, has recorded 800 cases of cures presumed to be miraculous. Among them are tuberculosis, blindness, meningitis, Pott's disease and cancer.

We append below a summary of the findings of Dr Mendes do Carmo, professor of theology at the seminary of Guarda, who was commissioned by the Bishop of Guarda to inquire into the extraordinary cure of Margarida Rebelo on May 13th, 1944, at Fatima. Dr Mendes do Carmo received the sworn testimony of doctors, nurses and witnesses, and the hospitals concerned placed their X-ray plates and files at his disposal.[2]

CURE OF MARGARIDA REBELO (1944)

(Paraplegia due to compression of the spinal cord; purulent cystitis, fistula formation)

Margarida de Jesus Rebelo was born in Guarda (Portugal) in 1921. She was orphaned of both parents at the age of fourteen.

On Christmas day, 1939, at the age of eighteen, she fell from a second story window; the fall left her unconscious. She was removed to bed and remained there for fifteen days. After this she got up, feeling quite well, complaining only of slight pain in the lumbar region of her back. This gradually became worse; a short course of diathermy relieved her only temporarily. However, the discomfort recurred, associated now with some difficulty in the movements of her lower limbs; as a result she fell several times while serving at table. Symptoms of disordered bowel and bladder function made their appearance.

In September 1941 the pains in the back became so severe as to be almost unbearable and weakness of the lower limbs now made walking impossible. From this time on she was confined to bed. Her lower limbs were now anaesthetic; urinary retention required an indwelling catheter and repeated washouts. She also suffered from rectal retention. She was at that time transferred to the hospital of Coimbra University where a plaster jacket was applied. She then returned to Guarda.

On February 16th, 1942, X-ray examination showed collapse of the body of the second lumbar vertebra, the apex of the collapsed bone pointing anteriorly. The vertebral body was displaced slightly backward. A new plaster casing was applied.

An X-ray report on March 19th, 1942, read: "Compression fracture of the body of the second lumbar vertebra; the bony changes being more prominent on the right side. The intervertebral discs between L1 and L2, and L2 and L3, are greatly narrowed. The backward displacement of the vertebral body is not serious."

On April 13th, 1942, she was admitted to Professor Angelo da Fonseca's wards. The case record contained the provisional diagnosis: "Old fracture of the second lumbar vertebra. Pain and paralysis(?)."

Her actual physical condition was, in general, good: she did not have a temperature. Pain was felt over the whole of the thoracic and lumbar spine. There were clear signs of gradual spinal cord compression. On examination, the genital adnexa were tender.

On April 15th an X-ray confirmed the previous one. April 16th W.R. was negative.

May 25th, urinary examination. "Pus 3+, occasional R.B.C. Large rounded epithelial cells. Many staphylococci; occasional bacilli. No tubercle bacilli (Koch), no hyaline, granular or epithelial casts, no crystals."

Treatment, at this point, included tetracoccus vaccine, urotropine, vitamin B_1. No undue temperature. In July, 1942, the plaster jacket was discarded as useless.

On September 29th another X-ray confirmed previous findings; it demonstrated no change in the bony structure of the broken bone.

In September, 1942, temperature was 38°C.; bladder washes were needed and coramine, dagenan and vitamin B_1 were given.

Temperature in October fluctuated between 38° and 39°C.; it fell in November, rose again in December and continued to swing till final cure.

On January 25th, 1943, the patient was taken back to the Guarda hospital where her suffering continued. Despite lack of clear evidence to support it, a diagnosis of Pott's disease was entertained and the advisability of sending the patient to a seaside sanatorium was considered.

At the end of April, 1944, the situation seemed grave; so grave, indeed, that when three small ulcers, discharging pus and apparently of a fistulous nature, appeared on the back, the nurses did not draw the doctor's attention to them, as the patient begged to be left in peace and there seemed no point in contradicting a dying woman.

On May 12th, 1944, the patient left for Fatima by railway sleeper. The journey was extremely burdensome, with much retching, pain and discomfort.

Dr Pereira Gens, medical director of the Sanctuary Hospital at Fatima, wrote at this stage: "She presented symptoms and signs of spinal cord compression, with pain in the lumbar region spreading all over the back, and anaesthesia and paralysis of the lower limbs and retention of urine needing a permanent indwelling catheter."

Dr Alfred Pimentel, helping the sick at Fatima, stated: "When I tried to examine Margarida Rebelo she showed herself unable to move at all. Paralysis was complete. The slightest pressure on the spinal column produced severe pain.

"Slight disuse atrophy (due to several months immobility) of the lower limbs was present. An indwelling urinary catheter for emptying the bladder was necessary, she suffered from disordered sphincteric activity with retention of urine and matter. She was intolerant to any food, including water."

With reference to the cystitis which had troubled her for three years, Irma Angelica, a nurse at the Guarda hospital, who had looked after her since September, 1943, stated: "I washed the patient completely on the night of her departure. I carried out the treatment of her bladder, which resulted in the passage of blood and pus." Dr Alfred Pimentel added to this: "She had a bladder wash-out during the night; the urine was thick and purulent, containing many semi-solid pieces of matter which obstructed the catheter."

The ulcers on the back were dressed before departure by Nurse Irma Angelica on May 12th. On May 13th, at midday, they were dressed again as the patient was suffering a great deal. This was done by Señorita Raymonde Grazieth da Salva, a former third-year medical student, who held a diploma in child-health, midwifery and care of the sick.

She stated: "I removed the dressing that covered three fistulae; on examination I found that two of these were superficial, one deep. The deep one was at the level of the second vertebra counting upward from the sacrum. The smell was most unpleasant. I passed an ordinary sound into it completely. I disinfected the small ones carefully with hydrogen peroxide. I did the same to the deep one with the help of a syringe, then pushed in a strip of gauze smeared with vaseline to ease its passage and then moistened it with hydrogen peroxide."

The state of affairs at this point may be summarised as follows:

1. Complete paralysis of lower limbs associated with anaesthesia existed; disordered sphincters and considerable backache were present.

Here was a syndrome associated with spinal cord compression, but this pressure effect could not have been caused by the fractured and backwardly displaced second lumbar vertebra. The spinal cord stops above the second lumbar vertebra; furthermore, a cord pressed upon by a displaced vertebra would not have taken a year to produce paralytic symptoms.

In view of these facts, a progressive compression was considered, possibly due to Pott's disease; a diagnosis unsupported by a most competent radiologist who supervised all the X-ray investigations. Two other possibilities may produce this syndrome—either an ascending pachymeningitis following the fracture, or a transverse myelitis secondary to macro- or micro-lesions in the cord produced at the time of the fall. The acute sensitivity complained of by the patient at the relevant level of her spinal cord favours this last hypothesis. Hysteria had been completely excluded by the doctors in attendance.

2. Obvious purulent cystitis, which necessitated a wash-out that night and morning.

3. A fistula about the size of a thumb and quite deep, dressed with gauze ribbon about midday on May 13th.

4. A running temperature of several months' duration.

5. Finally, the patient was moribund; her pulse was thready and uncountable (according to Dr Pimentel); she seemed to be dying.

At 2 p.m. the patient thought the end had come and was glad to be able to die at Our Lady's feet.

Shortly after this, as the blessing with the Sacred Host was being carried out, Margarida Rebelo experienced "something so astonishing that I don't know how to describe it. I felt completely cured, free of all pain. I wanted to get up and kneel before the Host, but the doctors would not let me."

Dr Pereira Gens states: "After the blessing of the sick, the orderly in charge of the patient came and told me that she claimed to be cured. I instructed the stretcher to be taken to the hospital where I went to see her almost immediately afterward. She was up and about, feeling very well, eating with gusto and chatting with those present. She moved freely in every way without pain. The cause of the spinal compression had suddenly disappeared."

The patient passed water naturally and the urine was clear and normal.

Señorita Raymonde Grazieth verified that the ulcers and fistula she had treated two hours previously had closed and there remained three scars just visible. "The gauze ribbon I had inserted into the deep and purulent fistula was clean. The whole dressing was clean, and free of smell or pus."

A subsequent X-ray showed no change in the fractured vertebral body.

The cure had apparently affected the pathological changes within the spinal cord or vertebral column responsible for the syndrome, also the urinary infection. The dorsal ulcers and the general disintegration of the patient's health had apparently instantaneously disappeared.

OUR LADY OF KNOCK

Knock is a little village in the diocese of Tuam in the west of Ireland. In 1879 fifteen people witnessed a rather complex apparition of Our Lady. A canonical court of inquiry sat for seven weeks on the incident and decided that their evidence, taken in its entirety, was satisfactory and reliable. Pilgrimages were organised and cures began to be reported.

A medical bureau, the Knock Shrine Medical Bureau, was set up in 1935 to investigate the cures.[3] Hospitals have been specially constructed to accommodate the sick. Additional buildings were opened in 1949. The *Knock Shrine Annual* is published yearly. The 1950 number reports numerous cures apart from those registered by the bureau.

Mr William D. Coyne, in his book *Cnoc Mhuire*,[4] reports several remarkable cures, of which we have chosen the cases of John O'Grady and John Kelly.

CURE OF JOHN O'GRADY (1925)
(Rachitic deformity of the legs)

"John O'Grady of Largan, Ballaghaderreen, County Roscommon, had been walking for a short time when he developed rickets and while still under two years lost the use of his feet altogether. A baby sister was then born and as there were nine in the family it was some time before the mother could take little John to the doctor. The late Dr Coen attended him and told his mother that he had rickets and his general health was so bad he did not think any treatment would be effective. The boy now became very delicate and there was not much hope for his recovery.[5]

"In December 1924 the mother took him to the Children's Hospital, Temple Street, Dublin, where he was treated for eight months. The doctors, the nurses and the sisters told the father who visited the child that while the boy's general health had much improved they could offer no hope for the recovery of his feet. At this time the shins were curved so badly, into hoop-shape, and the feet so deformed that the soles faced backward, leaving the child perfectly helpless.

"In this condition he was discharged as nothing more could be done. While at home the mother had to look after him as she would an infant. On September 3rd, 1925, after the usual hard day, which included outside work, as her husband was now earning in England, she felt too tired to give the child his usual bath. However, she found that other house needs had to be attended to and she could not get to bed before a late hour in any event. It then occurred to her for the first time to appeal to Our Lady of Knock for a cure for John. She remembered that the feast of the Nativity of the Blessed Virgin, September 8th, was near and having some holy water from Knock (which she got on her last visit there eight years before) she decided to bathe the child and on this occasion to use a spoonful of the holy water in the bath. Afterward the child was put to bed and went to sleep at once, but after about an hour he awoke in what seemed to be a violent spasm. He screamed and writhed as if in great pain. The mother and other children were terrified at the dreadful appearance presented by the contortions of the little boy and they felt he was dying. Everything possible was done to relieve and please him but he took no notice whatever of even the toys offered him. All the family were on their knees saying the rosary, and then the mother touched his lips with a crucifix (which she got at Knock also) and instantly the spasm ceased and the child smiled through his tears to her. Almost at once he went to sleep again and slept soundly until morning. Having dressed him and put him on his little stool, as was her custom, she went about her household work, when suddenly the other children called in great excitement, 'Mammy, Mammy, Johnnie is walking.' On turning she saw him, to her great amazement, actually running across the kitchen floor.

"He has walked unaided since then and is now a boy of

twenty-two, perfectly strong and healthy in every possible way, and takes his place in the outside work. His feet are quite straight and fully developed. (Interview with mother, March 1935.)"[6]

Cure of John Kelly (1929-1935)
(Genu valgum and Talipes valgus)

"On March 4th, 1935, Mrs Michael Kelly of Boleyard, Ballyvary, County Mayo, related the following account of the cure of her son.

"John was her youngest child and up to the age of five years he was not able to walk and never even attempted to stand, being a helpless child in his mother's arms. However, he had the full use of his speech and was wise beyond his years. He used to express great regret that he was not able to go around with his brothers and then he would not be such a burden on his mother, to whom he was deeply attached. Her slender means did not permit her to consult a doctor. At the age of two-and-a-half she first took the child to Knock, which is about fifteen miles from Boleyard. John's feet were then quite deformed and his whole body was becoming shapeless. On reaching Knock for the night-vigil of the feast of the Assumption the mother performed the full stations including the all-night prayer. There was no change. In the following year she returned to the shrine at the same time but again without result. Meanwhile, little Johnnie was getting worse. He was unable to sit up straight and his spine seemed to be weakening and his legs were reduced to skin and bone. The mother had deep devotion to Our Lady and she never lost hope. In this strong faith they both set out again for Knock for the third time, for the feast of the Assumption in the year 1929. The journey was a very difficult one and the mother had to carry the child all the way if she was not fortunate enough to get him carried by some neighbouring car or cart. Those who knew the hardship of the long journey discouraged her strongly, pointing out that there would be no cure when it did not come at the first visit. She was not to be put off. This time she had the company of some neighbours who kindly helped her to carry the child in turn. It was nearly dark on reaching Knock and without an interval for rest she visited the Blessed Sacrament with the child in her arms, and immediately performed the stations of the cross. The others begged her to rest herself as they felt she was over-taxing her strength. Tired and hot, she offered her extra sacrifice which she said would be pleasing to Our Lady, and continued her stations. At the third station the child suddenly cried out, "Oh Mother, Mother, let me down, I can walk." She was so excited that she immediately put him on the floor and to her complete astonishment he stood up, the first time in his life. He was able to walk round the church inside and did the outside stations with his mother three times afterward. He was then 5½ years old, and has since had the use of his feet. In the beginning his feet were out of shape and he did not have full power, but he improved rapidly each day. On the 8th of September following, she made a special visit of thanksgiving to Knock, alone, and on her return home that evening little John was the first to greet her some distance from the house and her gratitude was without bounds. Each year John and his mother, fulfilling a promise made to Our Lady, perform the vigil of prayer at Knock. Since he left school he has been working on the land in a perfectly normal manner.

"The following is Doctor Kirby's report:

" 'First examined on 15/8/29. A pronounced case of Genu valgum with associated Talipes valgus. His mother stated on that day that he had some hours previously walked for the first time in his life at the Catholic church, Knock. Scoliosis present and walked with difficulty.

" 'For the past six years received no surgical treatment. Examined 9/3/53, all trace of Talipes valgus and Genu valgum disappeared. Slight scoliosis present. I was amazed at his appearance on this occasion as he walked perfectly.

(signed) A. Kirby, M.D.' "[7]

OUR LADY OF POMPEII

This shrine owes its origin to the piety of Bartolo Longo, a lawyer, who in 1873 founded a confraternity in honour of Our Lady of the Rosary in the village of Valle di Pompeii. The devotion to Our Lady spread far and wide. A great basilica was built and large numbers of miraculous cures have been recorded, generally reported by the people concerned and corroborated by medical certificates. We present here the cases of Mother Falletta and Professor Vitelli.

CURE OF MOTHER M. A. FALLETTA (1940)

(*Cerebral tumour*)[8]

"After about two months' absence for sun-ray treatment, our superior, Mother M. Adalgisa Falletta, returned to Acireale in September, 1940, in a pitiable state: thin, pale, her eyes somewhat protruding, the pupils dilated, and complaining of severe headaches.

"We thought that the sun-baths had exhausted her, and that tonic treatment would build up her strength and gradually restore her to health. She had to wear blue-tinted spectacles to conceal her eyes from strangers. But in the days which followed she found that her sight was becoming rapidly weaker, until finally, one morning as she went up to the altar to receive Holy Communion, she tripped and fell on the steps. Her sight was completely gone. From that time she had to be accompanied everywhere. She suffered terrible headaches, but her confidence in God and Our Lady of Pompeii never wavered.

"On September 18th she was taken to Catania and examined by Professor Eugenio Aguglia, who observed notable exophthalmia with total bilateral external ophthalmoplegia.

"She became worse, and the pain became daily more severe, and she was taken once more to Catania on September 29th, where the professor found that her condition had deteriorated rapidly. The disease was far advanced and by now quite incurable.

"The feast of the Holy Rosary was approaching. About eleven o'clock in the evening of the vigil, we were reciting the fifteen mysteries of the rosary, and exactly at midnight, as is our custom, we began the Supplication. Even our sick mother, who had been brought in despite her fatigue, took part in this final prayer. As we came to the words 'this very day we look to you for the graces we desire' she began to see and was able to distinguish everything around her.

"Then she cried out, 'A miracle!' She rubbed her eyes in

great excitement, repeating, 'I can see, I can see, Our Lady has cured me!'

"Our joy was indescribable. Her eyes had returned to their normal state, she felt no more pain and was able to read the prayer of thanksgiving herself. A real wonder had taken place. . . ."

Medical Certificate

"On September 18th last year I examined Rev. Mother Adalgisa Falletta, of the Dominican Sisters of the Sacred Heart.

"I observed in particular exophthalmia with total bilateral external ophthalmoplegia.

"On September 29th I again examined the patient, whose condition had greatly and rapidly deteriorated. There was paralysis of the fourth and sixth nerves on both sides and almost total blindness. There were objective signs of increased intracranial pressure.

"The symptoms pointed inexorably to a diagnosis of cerebral tumour of the base.

"All symptoms of a hysterical nature can be ruled out in this case.

"Today, October 1st, Mother presented herself in my surgery completely cured.

"Such a cure, which took place instantaneously during the Supplication to Our Lady of Pompeii, cannot be accounted for by the natural laws governing the possible involution even of the gravest diseases, particularly in view of its having been instantaneous.

(Signed) Eugenio Aguglia, Professor."

CURE OF NATALE VITELLI (1948)

(Acute urinary infection)[9]

Medical Certificate

"I the undersigned, Dr Onofrio Costabile, doctor of medicine and surgery, certify that I have treated Professor Natale Vitelli, born and resident in Bosco-Trecase (Casavitelli district), suffering from acute cystitis complicated with urinary infection and septicæmia.

"His condition became gradually worse, despite the most careful attention, until early cardiac failure set in, which, in view of an almost total lack of nourishment for more than a fortnight, made all hope of a cure vain.

"I was assisted in my professional services by other local doctors and by specialists from the University of Naples, who all agreed that there was no possibility of recovery.

"I also certify that after the patient had received the last sacraments, when there was no further chance of saving his life, recourse was had to the intercession of Our Lady of Pompeii, and although no new treatment was tried, the patient's health began to improve from that moment and continued to do so daily until he was perfectly cured.

"In faith of which,

(Bosco-Trecase, 3/2/48)

(Signed) (Dr) Onofrio Costabile."[10]

OUR LADY OF LORETO

A well-known tradition has it that the house in which Our Lady lived in Nazareth was miraculously transported in 1291 to Tersato in Illyria, and then in 1294 to a spot not far from Ancona, on the Adriatic coast of Italy. It is now completely encased in marble and enshrined in a basilica built by the Popes of the fifteenth and sixteenth centuries. It contains a famous statue of Our Lady.[11]

This sanctuary has always had a great reputation for miracles attributed to the intercession of Our Lady of Loreto. The French writer Montaigne tells of the cure of a Parisian noble, Michel Marteau, Seigneur de la Chapelle, of an affliction of the leg, having heard the story in his own words.

Cures have occurred there in recent times. In 1939 the *Osservatore Romano* published one in particular which took place on July 2nd, 1938, and was examined by the College of Doctors of Loreto, Drs Carlo Sartori, Francesco Brancati, Rolando Girone, Umberto Mule, Lorenzo Guerrieri and Portini.

A large number of sanctuaries are recording cures in this way all over the world. Those we have mentioned have been singled out because each has its own supervisory medical organisation—the Fatima Medical Bureau, Knock Shrine Medical Bureau and the Loreto College of Doctors. It is to be hoped that they will in the future make an invaluable contribution to the medical study of miraculous cures. For our present purpose we have chosen the Lourdes Medical Bureau as the typical medical organisation of its kind. We discuss this organisation in detail in Chapter VI.

OUR LADY OF BEAURAING

We have seen how King Ezechias asked for a "physical" proof of the prophecy made to him by Isaias regarding his health, and how that proof was given. There are spiritual favours such as prophetical knowledge, visions, apparitions, known only to the favoured few, which are difficult to verify and require to be corroborated by concrete phenomena accessible to others. This corroboration is often supplied by miraculous cures. Those which have taken place at Lourdes or Fatima have certainly afforded no mean guarantee that the children's story of their apparitions was true.

A very interesting example of this is provided by what happened at Beauraing, in Belgium. Four children, aged between nine and fifteen years, claimed to have been favoured with apparitions of the Blessed Virgin between November 29th, 1932, and January 3rd, 1933. The affair gave rise to a good deal of controversy, especially among doctors, some admitting the reality of the apparitions and others rejecting them. The problem was complicated by the fact that the events of Beauraing had led to a minor epidemic of "apparitions" at that time.

Courts of inquiry were set up by the ecclesiastical authorities. Eventually, on December 7th, 1942, the Pope granted to the Bishop of Namur "faculties, as bishop of the place, to pass judgment on the facts as he saw fit, on his own authority and without in any way implicating the authority either of the Holy See or of the ecclesiastical province." Moreover, on January 9th, 1943, the president of the diocesan court of inquiry submitted to Mgr Charue, Bishop of Namur, a report which concluded thus: "The Commission considers that the diocesan authority could permit public devotion to Our Lady of Beauraing, without making any statement regarding the supernatural character of the facts."

The upshot was that Mgr Charue issued a decree on February 19th, 1949, authorising the cult of Our Lady of Beauraing, "in view of the fact that no cogent objection has been raised to the divine and supernatural character of what are called the apparitions of the Most Blessed Virgin to the children of Beauraing—on the contrary, the arguments in favour of their supernatural and divine character appear to be very solid, and have become all the more convincing with the passage of the years, considering also the tide of sincere and profound piety which for ten years has attracted the faithful to Beauraing, the numerous and often remarkable conversions—some of them stagger-ing—the many spiritual and other favours which flow from Beauraing, the perfect orthodoxy, the doctrinal appositeness and the power for good of what we may term the *message of Beauraing*."

But the decree made one thing clear: "Anxious to maintain the usual extreme prudence of the Church in these matters, we reserve our final judgment on the facts of Beauraing and on their nature."

For such a final judgment to be passed it was necessary to have proofs which positively compelled a decision.

With this in mind, it was decided to examine the cures attributed to Our Lady of Beauraing according to the procedure prescribed by canon law, that is to say the in-terrogation of a definite number of sworn witnesses (also sworn to secrecy), the checking of their evidence, the examination of the case by medical experts, final dis-cussions between the promoter of the faith and the advocate of the cause.

Two cases were selected by the doctrinal commission, that of Mademoiselle van Laer (Sister Pudentia) who was in all probability suffering from osteomyelitis, and that of Madame Acar, affected with myoma of the uterus.

We give below a summary of the experts' observations on these cases. It is worth mentioning that Mlle van Laer had already made five pilgrimages to Lourdes without success before she was cured at Beauraing. She was therefore used to pilgrimages, and not likely to be carried away by emotion or autosuggestion.

CASE OF MLLE VAN LAER (1933)

(*Osteomyelitis*)

The following statement, by Dr Picard and Dr Robaux, is relevant to this case:

"We, the undersigned, Dr Eugene Picard (lecturer in the University of Louvain, adviser in forensic medicine to the courts at Louvain) and Dr Albert Robaux (neurologist attached to the Institute of Beau-Vallon in Saint-Servais), summoned by the Beauraing commission, assembled in Namur, to give expert advice on the documents pertaining to the alleged extraordinary cure of Mlle van Laer (Rev. Sister Pudentia), having taken the oath, having already given our individual opinions, and having placed before the commission reports dated March 12th, 1949, and February 17th, 1949, respectively, in which we concluded that this cure could not be explained in natural terms, decided to meet at Rev. Fr Toussaint's office (the latter being an official member of the commission) to draw up an agreed statement on Mlle van Laer's case.

"Given that the patient's personal and family history are free of significant findings; given the description of the start of the illness (eczema-like rash on the inner aspect of the thighs and the perianal area, furuncles of the anal region and the legs, high temperature, severe headaches, especially around the eyes and ears, a history suggestive of serious generalised toxæmia associated with few local signs); given that the illness started at the age of seventeen; given that very large and painful abscesses soon formed in the region of the knee, which were followed by fistula formation in both the lower half of the calf and the area of the cervical vertebrae (multiple fistulae) and which were associated with quadriplegia; given the patient's condition from 1919 to 1928 (multiple suppurating abscesses over a period of nine to eleven years); we conclude: in view of the lesions in the cervical vertebrae and right leg (shown to us on X-ray plates); in view of the discharge of small pieces of bone from the leg, it seems certain that Mlle van Laer was afflicted with a serious infection, tuberculous or staphylococcal, in origin, and most probably a form of osteomyelitis.

"Although neither suppuration nor quadriplegia was present after 1930, it is clear that Mlle van Laer still suffered from the same illness on June 23rd, 1933. She remained afflicted by large swellings in the neck and right leg (the latter was twice as thick as the left) which were getting larger in the terminal months of her illness. These were inflammatory in nature, being extremely hard and not pitting on pressure. They could not be simply contractures, in view of the temperature the patient was running at this time (37.6 to 38°C., and sometimes more), and indicated the presence of an infectious process in one whose general condition was actually getting worse.

"In view of the diagnosis; in view of the patient's temperament, which does not suggest nervousness or hysteria; in view of the treatment applied at the relevant times (sedative or stimulant drugs of a general nature); in view of the swiftness of the patient's cure (one night only), a cure which must be considered complete in view of the absence of relapse over a period of sixteen years despite the heavy work she had to do throughout the war period; we state and have stated that we cannot explain in simply natural terms the disappearance of the functional impairment and of the neck and leg swellings; we consider psychological factors able to account only for the sudden disappearance of the pains, and the sudden improvement of the general condition.

"Given the unusual nature of these facts, and the bearing they may have on the events at Beauraing, we consider that these documents and reports should be handed to the diocesan

E

commission so that they may pursue the investigation of the matter in the light of the known facts.

(Signed) E. Picard. A. Robaux.
Jambes, March 27th, 1949."

Case of Mme Acar (1933)
(Myoma of uterus)

The following statement by Dr A. Docquier, May 8th, 1949, is relevant to this case:

"Mme Acar's history may be summarised as follows: spontaneous, swift and absolute disappearance of a voluminous pelvic tumour with return to complete health of the patient.

"The tumour's existence is established by Dr van de Putte's investigations. The diagnosis of uterine myoma is established by the shape of the growth (regular), its consistency (moderately hard), its site (median), its continuity with the cervix uteri and the presence of considerable blood loss.

"Strictly speaking, the differential diagnosis of ovarian cyst ought to be considered, though in general such cysts are not situated in the median line, nor continuous with the cervix uteri nor accompanied by bleeding.

"On the other hand two further possible diagnoses may be confidently set aside; firstly, that of pregnancy, on account of the length of time (two years) the tumour took to develop (its growth was recorded by Dr van de Putte), and also on account of the free recurrent bleeding. Secondly, a diagnosis of fibrous polyp may be discarded; while such growths can reach considerable size, they usually (especially if they reach any significant size) dilate the cervix uteri and become palpable through the open external os; in this case the growth was continuous with the cervix.

"Dr van de Putte recorded the disappearance of the tumour. This was rapid. [Subjectively the cure occurred on the evening of July 30th, 1933. It was complete the next day as judged by absence of discharge on the dressings. Normal periods started twenty-eight days later and recurred in September. The ex-patient, then quite sure of her recovery, saw Dr van de Putte to have the matter verified. (Canon Monin, loc. cit., p. 154) Dr van de Putte had seen the patient with her large tumour;

two months later he saw her again and records that her uterus was now of an infantile type. This change had occurred quite spontaneously, no surgical, radiotherapeutic or medical treatment having been applied.]

"Mme Acar's health has returned to normal, secondary gastric symptoms have disappeared and, most important, normal and regular periods have been re-established.

"The disappearance of the growth may be explained naturally in three ways:

"If it were a case of spontaneous absorption of a myoma at the menopause. However, a tumour of this size does not vanish in two months; nor was Mme Acar menopausal, as she continued to menstruate normally after the tumour's disappearance.

"If it were a case of pregnancy—an untenable hypothesis (see above).

"If it were a case of spontaneous evacuation of a necrosed fibrous polyp; an untenable hypothesis (see above). Finally, if the case were one of ovarian cyst, how could its complete, sudden and spontaneous disappearance be explained?

"Conclusion. From my investigation of the case notes of Mme Acar and subsequent discussion, I am of the opinion that the spontaneous, rapid and complete disappearance of growth afflicting her cannot, in the present state of medical science, be explained as due to natural causes.

(Signed) A. Docquier."

Statement by Dr Renaer, May 15th, 1949:

"I, the undersigned, Dr Marcelin-Joseph Renaer, lecturer in the University of Louvain, having sworn to treat as secret the case notes given to me on May 11th, 1949, by Rev. Fr F. Toussaint, promoter of the faith in the Acar case, examining the matter purely from the medical point of view, leaving the juridical and historical aspects of the case to the diocesan commission of Namur, give as my opinion the following hypothesis regarding the Acar case:

1. "The facts given might suggest in the differential diagnosis a case of chronic inflammation of the uterine adnexa. This diagnosis is not supported by the observations that:

"The tumour formed an anatomical whole without lateral

expansions, continuous with the cervix uteri. (Cf. q. 2, questionnaire of April 13th, 1949.) The tumour was continuous with the cervix uteri and no nodules or palpable lumps could be detected. (Cf. letter dated April 6th, 1949, number 5.)

"Menorrhagia occurred for several months.

2. "The same difficulties present themselves in consideration of an ovarian cyst. The facts that the growth formed an anatomical whole and that menorrhagia was present lead me to the same conclusion as that made in (1) above.

3. "A cystic fibroma might be considered in view of Dr van de Putte's finding that the tumour was 'not hard.' Even if this were the case, the problem remains unaltered as we are then simply dealing with a complication in the development of a fibromyoma.

4. "The possibility of a submucous fibroma (fibrous polyp) which was progressively expelled after necrosing is unlikely in view of the fact that continuous blood loss is not recorded. Furthermore, it would not be expelled in toto. In addition Dr van de Putte found an infantile uterus at the end of September, 1933, two months after the pilgrimage. (Cf. q. 15, questionnaire 1.)

5. "The possibility of a dead ovum which was ultimately suddenly or gradually expelled remains. However:

"There is no question of amenorrhœa or likelihood of pregnancy.

"No mass was expelled, a fact which would have been apparent to Mme Acar, given that the uterus was the size of a child's head (Dr van de Putte's certificate, dated March 6th, 1934).

"The fact that the menorrhagia recurred so often does not fit in with a diagnosis of a dead ovum.

"The question of pain, though a subjective phenomenon, deserves special examination. The pain was generally gastric in site; it was worse after a meal. The patient suffered from cramps, particularly after food. These facts seem to me to suggest that the pains had no direct relationship with the pelvic disorder and therefore they have no diagnostic value.

"There remains Dr van de Putte's diagnosis of a uterine

fibroma; this cannot be set aside, both objective and subjective findings confirming the diagnosis.

"Assuming that the diagnosis is one of fibroma, one which I am prepared to support if the depositions in the case notes are to be relied upon, the change in two or three months' time of a uterine fibroma seven to eight inches in diameter (the size of a child's head) into an infantile uterus cannot be explained in natural terms in view of the fact that the menopause occurred five years later.

(Signed) M. Renaer."

[After discussing these reports and the contents of the case files, the commission came to the conclusion that it was possible "without imprudence, to attribute these cures to the all-powerful intervention of Our Lady of Beauraing," and decided to submit the case notes, reports and conclusions to the judgment of the diocesan authority. As a result, on July 2nd, 1949, Monsignor Charue promulgated a decree, stating:]

"We have judged and do judge, have declared and do declare that the cures of Mlle van Laer and Mme Acar are miraculous; and that, in view of the circumstances in which they occurred, they can be attributed to God's special intervention, through the intercession of Our Lady of Beauraing."

The bishop then addressed a letter, similarly dated, to the diocesan clergy, as follows:

"Venerable and dear brethren,

"The decree you have just read marks a decisive moment in the history of the cult of Our Lady of Beauraing.

"As you know, when we first took official cognisance of this cult, our statement contained certain clear reservations; we did not consider that the time was ripe to declare ourselves 'on the reality and supernatural nature of the phenomena.' Since then the motives prompting us to put it off have become weaker and weaker, and we may now say, before God, that evidence is no longer wanting to convince us personally of the frail nature of the prudent reserve expressed by us in the beginning. We awaited the time when we could publicly take the final step. We consider this hour has come. The happy issue of the diocesan commission's labours has enabled us to declare as miraculous two of the cures obtained by the intercession of Our Lady of Beauraing. Occurring in the months succeeding the phenomena of Beauraing, accompanied by other cases of spiritual and temporal favours, and based upon a surge of devotion to Mary which has continued to this day, these miraculous cures constitute the ultimate proofs to convince us of the supernatural nature of the phenomena.

"Giving thanks to God and the Most Holy Virgin, we can with prudence and confidence declare that the Queen of Heaven appeared to the children of Beauraing during the winter of 1932-33, to give us a special token of her maternal love, to make an earnest call to prayer and to assure us of her powerful intervention for the conversion of sinners."

It will be appreciated from the above that (without becoming articles of faith) presumably miraculous cures can reasonably be regarded as evidence for the validity of spiritual phenomena and contribute to the recognition of a general or local cult.

MIRACLES ASSOCIATED WITH HOLY PERSONS

Our Lord gave His apostles power to heal the sick, and the Acts of the Apostles tells us that they used to bring the sick out into the streets in the hope that St Peter's shadow would fall upon them and cure them as they passed by (Acts 5, 15). Among a host of others, St Vincent Ferrer in the fifteenth century was a great miracle-worker who seemed to sow cures wherever he went.

The twentieth century is in no way lacking in examples of this extraordinary grace being granted to certain individuals. Strangely enough, it is the ultra-modern continent of America which provides two of them, one in the north, Brother Andrew in Canada, and the other in the south, Father Eustace in Brazil.

*   *   *

BROTHER ANDREW (1845-1937)[12]

Alfred Bessette, after having been in turn cobbler, blacksmith, farm hand and factory worker, in 1870 entered the

Congregation of the Holy Cross as a lay brother under the name of Brother Andrew. He carried out the duties of porter in the College of Notre Dame at Montreal. He had a special devotion to St Joseph. Before long his life became a series of wonders. A little oil in a lamp burning before the statue of St Joseph, a novena, a prayer, a word, and the sick were healed of their infirmities. His porter's lodge was besieged, the children's parents objected to this invasion of the school, the superiors were displeased, the medical officer of health became anxious . . . and the cures continued. And through the patient, untiring efforts of the humble brother, a chapel, then a basilica was built in honour of St Joseph. The cures multiplied, and when Brother Andrew died he was at the height of his fame.

A canonical inquiry is in progress, so we are not in a position to dwell on his life and extraordinary cures. We hope that the whole story will soon be made available to our scientific curiosity and veneration.

FATHER EUSTACE (1890-1943)[13]

Hubert van Lieshout was born in Holland in 1890. From the first he wanted to be a missionary, and he joined the Congregation of the Sacred Heart, commonly known as the Picpus Fathers. He was ordained priest as Father Eustace in 1919. A man of prayer, zeal and fiery ardour, he led a hard apostolic life, first in Holland and then, from 1925 onward, in Brazil. It appears that the gift of miracles only came to him later, in 1940, when he was parish priest of Poa in the district of São Paulo.

To counteract the activities of the spiritists, who used to distribute medicinal water, he began to distribute Lourdes water, and when that was exhausted, he blessed the water in his well. . . . Cures were worked, and a flood of invalids began to arrive. Thousands and thousands of people flocked to him in search of the miraculous blessing. When he went to São Paulo crowds of the faithful blocked the streets and stopped the traffic. Both civil and religious authorities were alarmed. He was transferred elsewhere, but wherever he went, the "miracles" followed.

He was threatened with interdict. It was then that he described the mission which, he said, God had given him. In a long letter to the Archbishop of São Paulo, he wrote: ". . . God has visibly shown me the path I must tread. . . . What can I say of this gift which God in His mercy has given me, a poor sinner? Matter is the way which leads to the spiritual . . . bodily cures are merely a means to obtain a far more important cure, the healing of souls, not only those of the people cured, but also of the bystanders. That is the holy calling I feel within me: to restore the faith by works of faith."

His wandering, eventful life continued, until on August 30th, 1943, he died of typhus at Bello Horizonte. His funeral was a triumphal procession. The archbishop presided and members of the government claimed the honour of carrying his coffin. And at his grave the wonders go on. . . .

Here again the ecclesiastical authorities are sifting the evidence, subjecting it to a minute and careful scrutiny. Hence the documents required to judge the cures attributed to the wonder-worker are not yet at our disposal.

But one thing we must say: the ecclesiastical authorities will concern themselves with the question of the sanctity and the miracles worked after the death of a servant of God, but as a general rule no final decision will be made until at least fifty years afterward. That means that cures attributed to miracle-workers have practically no official value and are not subject to immediate investigation, as is desirable not only from the scientific point of view, but also, it would seem, from the theological.

Doubtless among the crowds of "cures" there must be cures of more or less imaginary diseases, and imaginary cures of really sick people, who after a moment of exaltation fall back into their life of suffering. There must also be cures of functional or nervous disorders (many of which may be genuinely miraculous). But among them there are sure to be organic cures capable of scientific verification. Among the cures attributed to Father Eustace it is said that a case of tuberculosis of the bone in a very advanced stage was cured under the very eyes of the doctors at the time of his departure from Poa.

However, the following deposition may be worth recording:

CASE OF HELENA LOBOSQUE (1940)
(*Acute dermatitis consequent on erysipelas*).

"I, Helena Lobosque, living in São Paulo, declare that in the year 1940 I was seriously ill with erysipelas in the legs.

"I consulted many doctors, among whom I may mention my son Pasquale. My son, impressed by the case, brought to the house several of his colleagues whom I know to be leaders of the medical profession and specialists in diseases of the skin.

"On examination they found my case very peculiar because the erysipelas was constantly spreading, reducing my legs to two open wounds.

"I realised that only a miracle could save me. With this in mind I asked Father Eustace to give me his blessing.

"I began to feel well at once, and three days later I had recovered completely. Words cannot express my great happiness at being once more on my feet. . . .
São Paulo, 26/10/43.
　　　　(Signed) Helen Lobosque.　Dr P. Lobosque."

We consider it deplorable, from the point of view of "Catholic medicine," that is, of medicine which takes into account all the forces bearing on the human organism, the supernatural factors included, that such cures are not checked, examined, described and discussed before Catholic medical societies, and published too, if need be, in order to further both our scientific knowledge and at the same time our admiration for and gratitude to God. There should not merely be medical bureaux attached to a few sanctuaries—every Catholic doctor (and why not the others as well?) should have it at heart to form part of a world-wide medical bureau.

CASE OF CHARBEL MAKHLOUF[14]

The case of Charbel Makhlouf forms a link between those who work miracles in their lifetime and the holy people whose sanctity is manifested by cures after their death. He was a Maronite monk who died in 1898 after a life of remarkable virtue and austerity. It seems that some favours were granted while he was alive, but it was not until April 1950, half a century after his death, that astonishing cures began to take place at his grave, which has become a centre of pilgrimage for Christians and Moslems alike. His cause has been introduced in Rome, and on August 4th, 1950, in the presence of Mgr Tardini and Mgr Trafia, representing the Holy See, his body was exhumed and found to be wonderfully preserved.

CURE OF BECHARA ANTOUN ROUHANA (1950)
(Ankylosis of the foot caused by tuberculous osteitis)
Medical Certificate.

"I, the undersigned, Dr Joseph Farhat, director of public assistance in the Lebanon, certify as follows:

"Bechara Antoun Rouhana, aged thirty-seven years, labourer domiciled in the village of Jage, Lebanon, seven years ago contracted tuberculous osteoarthritis of the instep with open suppuration on both sides, internal and external. The lesion was confirmed by X-ray. His foot was put in plaster at the Hospital of Lebanon in a state of flexion, in order to produce ankylosis in a position which would enable him to walk. Holes were left in the plaster so that the suppurating ulcerations could be dressed. Several days after this he left the hospital and returned home.

"During the winter there was no doctor in his village. He had, therefore, to look after the dressings himself, but this he did so inexpertly that the plaster was soon drenched with pus and became so unbearable that he split it open from top to bottom, transforming it into a gutter which he took off for the dressings and put on again afterward.

"The plaster, thus loosened, could no longer immobilise the foot. It did become ankylosed in time, but in a state of complete extension, so that in spite of the cure of the tuberculous lesion, the patient could not put his foot flat on the ground but only touch it with his toes. The foot was quite useless and he had to drag himself about on crutches.

"When I returned to Beirut two years ago, I brought him to see Dr Fruchaud, a famous French specialist in diseases of the bone. The great surgeon decided that a surgical operation was necessary to reset the foot—a bloody business—after which it would have to remain in plaster for three or four months to produce ankylosis in the required position.

"The patient decided to undergo the operation and returned home in order to sell a strip of land to pay for it.

"Two years went by, and still he could not find a buyer. He led a sad and hopeless existence, for he was the father of a family, yet unable to do anything for them. Then he heard of the miraculous doings of the saintly Father Charbel. He went to visit him. He knelt down at his graveside. . . . In less than a quarter of an hour he rose to his feet, cured. He left his crutches at the monastery and walked home, a distance of over six miles.

"When I heard the news I went to Jage to see for myself. What was my astonishment to find that this man, hitherto unable to walk, had recovered eighty per cent of the use of his foot.

"Not only does he walk without crutches, but even without a stick. He is doing the same work as before he fell ill, digging and tilling the soil. He still limps slightly, but that does not inconvenience him in walking or working.

"This fact can only be explained by supernatural agency, since the ankylosis, produced by an organic process of consolidation, was irreducible by natural means. Even the proposed operation held out no hope of a cure, but merely the transformation of the existing ankylosis into one less crippling.

"In faith of which, this present certificate is made out.
Beirut, 29/6/50

(Signed) Dr Farhat "

PRIVATE CURES

These are cures which take place quite simply in homes and hospitals as the result of prayers and acts of devotion. Naturally cures worked in connection with various shrines can also happen in this way, privately.

To all appearances the disease was incurable, fatal; but suddenly all is well. The doctor is a little surprised and congratulates himself on the success of his treatment. The family timidly suggests that perhaps it was a miracle. The doctor shrugs his shoulders, or smiles and says, "Just so, just so; that's quite a possibility, isn't it?" Nevertheless, there are not many doctors who, in the course of their professional career, have not encountered some surprising case in which a little more accuracy of diagnosis, a more objective observation of the development of the disease, a more careful check on the circumstances of the cure might have revealed really extraordinary facts pointing to the hand of God. But all too frequently the matter is left there. Perhaps the doctor may confide to a friendly colleague. "The other day I had a queer sort of case . . ."

But no man of science has any right to remain indifferent to "a queer sort of case." The words reveal either a gap in our knowledge or perhaps the intervention of God. In the first assumption, the gap must be filled, if possible; in the second, surely a scientific mind should look for some explanation, and try to find out *how* it happened.

There is no need to belabour the point. What has been said or will be said in this book about the characteristics of miraculous cures, together with the examples quoted, will naturally provide an indication how to proceed in the investigation of a private cure apparently due to supernatural agency. We may simply remark that we ourselves have had to do with such cases.

The following report published by Dr Ausems, surgeon in the St Anthony Hospital, Utrecht, in the October 1926 number of *R. K. Artsenblad* is of interest:

CURE OF VROUW O. H—— (1926)

(Malignant chorionepithelioma with metastases)

"At the beginning of April, 1926, Vrouw O. H—— of Windschoote, twenty-nine years of age, mother of four children, had a miscarriage after about two months, which at first appeared to develop along normal lines. But the flow of blood, which had stopped after some days, began again and continued. It was then (early in June) that I was called in as consultant to examine the patient. Her doctor informed me by letter that the miscarriage had in fact been an abortion of a mole, and when I had examined the uterus and found it enlarged and soft, I suspected a chorionepithelioma and had the patient brought into my wards at the St Anthony Hospital, Utrecht.

"I conducted a more detailed examination several days later. She already looked very ill, and my fears increased when she told me she had been spitting blood for some days, and I suspected a pulmonary metastasis. At my request a specialist, Dr. Boekelman, examined her lungs and detected a rattle in several places as well as zones of respiratory obscurity. Radioscopic examination told the same story, revealing extensive shaded areas on both lungs.

"Curettage of the uterus, then a little bigger than a large orange, was carried out, and a considerable number of large bleeding granulations were removed from the cavity. In view of the danger of uterine perforation and of the certainty of the diagnosis, the uterus was not completely emptied. A further fact served to aggravate the prognosis—at the vaginal orifice a tumour was observed as big as a horse chestnut and blackish-brown in colour.

"It was therefore a chorionepithelioma with vaginal propagation and widespread pulmonary metastases. The diagnosis meant that there was no hope of successful therapeutic treatment and the prognosis was certain death in a matter of weeks, or months at most. Moreover, since the pulmonary condition had been detected her general health had deteriorated rapidly, and during the eight or ten days she remained in the hospital this woman—still young and comparatively well on her arrival—wasted visibly, lost all her strength and ran a high temperature every day.

"The patient returned home in this wretched condition, and her doctor, Dr Bougard, of Windschoote, was informed of the fatal prognosis. Her family were also told and soon began to expect the worst as she sank daily lower and lower.

"Her near relations then began a novena in honour of St Theresa of Lisieux. On the ninth day, when the sick woman had long ceased to take any more medicine, the downward progress was halted and her condition remained stationary. This initial success prompted the family to undertake a second novena. This was done, and even before it was completed all uterine loss of blood had disappeared and those around her realised that she was getting steadily better.

"A week or two later I received a letter from her doctor—who was not a Catholic—telling me that our patient was improving and that she was spitting blood at less frequent intervals. He admitted that he could not understand it, asked for my advice and invited me to examine her afresh.

"This examination did not take place immediately, but on September 20th, 1926.

"I then beheld a fine strapping young woman, the picture of health, robust and blooming in appearance. She did her own housework without fatigue, she had put on a good deal of weight and no longer spat either blood or anything else. No further loss of blood had appeared. Her period had occurred normally a fortnight previously, for the first time since her pregnancy. The uterus was in anteflexion and perfectly normal in size, shape and consistency. There was nothing unusual at the level of the adnexa and the vaginal tumour had disappeared entirely. A clinical examination of the lungs carried out by Dr Boekelman revealed no pathological symptoms whatever.

"To make assurance doubly sure an X-ray was taken and the lungs were found to be normal."

Dr Ausems concludes that this cure can only be explained by a miracle. (His conclusion is, of course, binding on no one.) The translators have experienced a similar sort of case, although the diagnosis was less clear-cut. At first we were inclined to hold that it would be wiser to say that our cure could perhaps have a natural explanation, but the subsequent history of the case, gradually cured and under treatment, has led to a slowly growing conviction that a miraculous intervention may have occurred at one point. See Appendix [1].

CHAPTER IV

CHURCH PROCEDURE FOR
INVESTIGATING MIRACULOUS CURES[1]

The Sacred Congregation of Rites is the organisation charged with checking and investigating miraculous cures. The earliest traces of the Roman congregations are to be found in the *Presbyterium* of the primitive Church, a sort of council which assisted the Pope in the government of the Church. This Presbyterium, composed of the suburban bishops together with the priests and deacons of the city of Rome, is mentioned as early as the third century, in the pontificate of Pope St Cornelius. Later, from the ninth century onward, the original Presbyterium was replaced by the Roman councils, and matters of exceptional difficulty were dealt with in *consistory* or in *commissions* set up for the purpose.

In the thirteenth and fourteenth centuries the tribunals, like the Rota and the Penitentiary, made their appearance, with the task of handling causes specially entrusted to them by the Pope. Finally, the sixteenth century saw the rise of the Roman congregations, the earliest in date being that of the Inquisition, founded by Pope Paul III. Others followed soon after under Paul IV, Pius V and Gregory XIII. But the chief architect and organiser of the congregations was Sixtus V (1585-1590) who raised their number to fifteen and assigned to each its own duties and prerogatives. The full tally of the congregations was later completed by Gregory XV, Urban VIII, Clement IX and Pius VII.

Saint Pius X completely reorganised the Roman Curia and made the congregations quite distinct in their scope from the tribunals. The former were henceforth to deal exclusively with administrative matters. However, the

Congregations of the Holy Office, of Rites and of the Sacraments do occasionally form special tribunals and try crimes against the faith, causes of beatification and canonisation, and certain marriage cases respectively.

The Congregation of Rites was established by Sixtus V in 1588. Its prefect is a cardinal, assisted by a secretary (who is usually a titular archbishop) and several other officials. A certain number of cardinals are members of the congregation and are assisted by a host of consultors. The headquarters of the congregation are now in the Palace of the Congregations in the Trastevere quarter of Rome. The Code of Canon Law describes the functions of the congregation in canon 253: "The Sacred Congregation of Rites has the right to examine and to decide all matters directly concerned with the sacred rites and ceremonies of the Latin Church . . . Its chief duties are therefore to see that the sacred rites and ceremonies are properly observed in the celebration of Mass, in the administration of the Sacraments, in the performance of the divine offices and in everything pertaining to the worship of the Latin Church; to grant appropriate dispensations; to confer insignia and privileges *honoris causa* . . . connected with the sacred rites and ceremonies, and to ensure that no abuses creep in in this respect. Finally, its competence extends to all that in any way concerns the beatification and canonisation of the servants of God as well as sacred relics."

The Church has always reserved to her own authority decisions regarding her public worship. But the history of her discipline in this matter can be divided into several distinct periods. The first extends from earliest times to the reign of Alexander III in the twelfth century. A public cultus was paid at first to the martyrs, then to other confessors, with the bishop's approval in each case. It was an official but local devotion and was more or less equivalent to what is now called beatification.

F

The second period stretches from the pontificate of Alexander III to those of Sixtus V and Urban VIII (1623-1644). Alexander III laid down that the examination of causes of beatification should henceforth be the business of the Holy See alone. Sixtus V in his constitution of January 22nd, 1588, setting up the Sacred Congregation of Rites, declared that it was to "preside with diligence over the canonisations of saints," at the same time conferring upon it power to regulate procedure. Urban VIII clarified and perfected this procedure, the object of which was to investigate and certify the martyrdom, virtues and miracles of the servants of God.

A third phase was begun by the celebrated canonist Prospero Lambertini who became Pope Benedict XIV (1740-1758). Before his elevation to the papacy, while still a professor of canon law, he had written the masterly treatise "De Beatificatione et Canonizatione Servorum Dei," which may rightly be called the Magna Carta of beatification and canonisation processes. The Code of Canon Law published by Pope Benedict XV in 1917 reproduces with minor alterations the work of Benedict XIV on the methods to be employed in these processes.

BEATIFICATION AND CANONISATION PROCEDURE[2]

Every beatification or canonisation presupposes a process, either *ordinary* (*per viam noncultus*, i.e., where there is no public devotion) or *extraordinary* (*per viam casus excepti vel cultus*, i.e., founded on public devotion). This fundamental distinction is derived from a decree of the Holy Office dated 1625 which exempts from the ordinary procedure certain cases where a legitimate public cultus already exists.

EXTRAORDINARY PROCEDURE. The extraordinary or exceptional procedure was formerly called "equivalent beatification or canonisation" (*beatificatio aequipollens*).

The Code of Canon Law makes no mention of the term. Nevertheless inclusion in the Roman Missal of the feasts of servants of God venerated in certain countries or religious orders without their cultus having been officially extended to the Universal Church, has always been called "equivalent canonisation" because from the liturgical point of view it has exactly the same effects as solemn canonisation. Usually this insertion is carried out by a simple decree of the Sacred Congregation of Rites. For example, Pius XI on December 16th, 1931, extended to the whole Latin Church the office and Mass of Albert the Great (d. 1280) by a papal bull in which he describes his action as an equivalent canonisation.

ORDINARY PROCEDURE. Although every member of the Church has the right to ask that a cause be introduced, this is usually done by a group (of priests or lay people) in some way connected with the candidate for beatification, or by the religious community to which he belonged. The request is made in writing, in the form of an introductory letter (or 'libel') addressed to the competent authority, the bishop of the place. The bishop is under no obligation to make any further move in the matter if he decides that the case does not warrant it. But if the request is accepted, the prescribed procedure is set in motion and the applicant chooses a postulator (who must be resident in Rome) to act in his name. The postulator's function is to present the cause before the competent judges and to carry out the various duties required by law. His chief task is to draw up the "articles" (*positiones*) in which the facts to be proved are set forth. These consist in short numbered statements introduced by the formula: "It is the truth that . . ."

In causes dealt with by the sacred congregation one of the cardinal members of the congregation is detailed by the Pope to undertake the duties of *"ponens"* or spokesman. It is his task to make a detailed study of the cause entrusted to him and to submit a report upon everything in its favour or otherwise to the plenary or ordinary meeting.

A promoter of the faith must take part in each process. The promoter of the faith attached to the sacred congregation is called the promoter-general of the faith. The assessor of the congregation, who assists him, is called the sub-promoter-general of the faith. Both are nominated by the Pope. In local tribunals it is the bishop who designates the promoter of the faith, except in apostolic processes. His function is to defend the law. To this end he draws up questionnaires of a factual character, the object of which is to bring to light the facts of the case. He also has power to insist that extra witnesses be called *ex officio* and to make such objections to their evidence as may seem opportune.

A notary or secretary must be present at every process, ordinary or apostolic, and his signature at the foot of the minutes is a necessary condition of their validity. In causes of beatification and canonisation these must be written out entirely *by hand*, to ensure their perfect preservation. The notary serving the sacred congregation must belong to the College of Apostolic Protonotaries.

The advocates and procurators in beatification causes heard before the sacred congregation must be doctors of canon law and at least licentiates of theology, and have served an apprenticeship with one of the advocates of the congregation. In addition advocates must have gained the diploma of Rotal Advocate.

There are in existence well-defined general rules covering the proofs required.

Absolute proof is essential. Canon 2019 of the code says that "in these causes (i.e. of beatification) the proofs must be altogether complete; and no other form of proof will be admitted except that derived from witnesses or documents." By 'complete proofs' are understood those which leave no room for doubt. To them is contrasted the *adminiculum* or confirmatory proof. However, a number of these may be combined in a particular case so as to provide complete proof.

The prescriptions of the canon law regarding the number and character of the witnesses required for complete proof in the various stages of the cause are as follows:

(1) In proof of absence of cultus, at least four witnesses are needed to establish that no public devotion was ever paid to the servant of God.

(2) In order to guarantee the fame of the virtues, martyrdom and miracles of a servant of God, at least ten witnesses are required, two of them called *ex officio*, Contemporary evidence must be that of eyewitnesses. In very old causes they can merely testify that the reputation for sanctity still persists. As for the detailed proof of the virtues or martyrdom, the Sacred Congregation of Rites distinguishes various types of witness: eyewitnesses, witnesses by word of mouth (*ex auditu*), who have only heard about the facts of which they speak, and witnesses by public knowledge (*ex publica fama*), who can merely testify to an existing tradition. Witnesses *ex auditu* are in turn divided into two categories according as they have heard of the facts from eyewitnesses (*ex auditu a videntibus*) or from others not eyewitnesses (*ex auditu auditus*).

Canon 2020 (3) lays it down as a principle that eyewitnesses and co-witnesses are required to provide proof of the virtues and martyrdom. Historical documents merely serve to consolidate the proof. Co-witnesses are those named by the witnesses as having had the same experiences as their own. This principle finds its application in canon 2020 (4) and (5): "If there are witnesses deriving their information from eyewitnesses in the apostolic process, and eyewitnesses in the (diocesan) informative process, these may be combined to provide proof."

If those giving evidence in the informative process were eyewitnesses, and those in the apostolic process merely heard the facts from others who were not eyewitnesses, the value of the latter is merely corroborative, greater or less according to the judgment of the court. Nor can the process (i.e. the discussion of the miracles) be continued unless the evidence hangs together in such a way that it acquires a probative force sufficient to convince a prudent man faced with a grave decision. On the other hand, in ancient causes based on absence of cultus, in which eyewitnesses are not available, proof may be led for the virtues and martyrdom by means of witnesses who have heard of the facts, or of witnesses to an unbroken tradition and of contemporary documents or monuments recognised as authentic. With regard to these ancient causes it may be observed that the Sacred Congregation of Rites, in a decree dated 1741, lays down the proviso that delay in opening the informative process was not due to fraud—for example, because it was put off until the death of certain inconvenient witnesses or through negligence.

(3) As canon 2020 (7) lays down, "Miracles must always be proved by the evidence of eyewitnesses and co-witnesses." No good is, therefore, served by bringing up marvels worked in the dim past, which can only be attested by others than eyewitnesses or by historical documents.

(4) Urban VIII, in a constitution dated July 5th, 1634, decreed that henceforward only those instances of cultus dating at least from 1534, and guaranteed by an unbroken popular tradition, would be sanctioned by the Church.

There are also particular rules covering the proofs required.

(1) The court must first receive evidence from all those who were in constant touch with the servant of God, for reasons of family, friendship or affection, or simply because they lived in the immediate neighbourhood.

A decree of the Sacred Congregation of Rites issued on August 26th, 1913, requires, under pain of nullity of the informative process, that those should be heard in the second place who wish to give evidence against the cause, not just in a vague general manner, but about a particular fact known to them, which throws an unfavourable light on the cause.

When the miracles are under consideration, the doctors concerned must be called, not as experts but as witnesses. If they refuse to give evidence before the court, the judge must try to induce them to draw up a report on the disease and its progress (in writing and under oath) and then have it embodied in the minutes. If this cannot be done he should at least endeavour to obtain their opinions by means of a third party, who will then be called to give evidence. From this it is clear what importance is attached to the evidence of the doctors treating the case.

The witnesses must give the reasons why they are sure of the truth of their statements, otherwise their evidence will be held as valueless. In other words, it is not enough for a witness to declare his conviction that the servant of God practised this virtue or that—for then proof would be too easy—but he must indicate the facts on which his conviction is based. In the same way, in order to avoid all suspicion of partiality on the part of the witnesses, canon 2030 demands that where the reputation for sanctity or the martyrdom of a servant of God belonging to a religious congregation is under review, half of the witnesses must not be members of that body. Since the minimum number of witnesses required in the informative process is ten, that means that at least five must not belong to the congregation of the servant of God. This restriction applies to the informative process alone, but even in the apostolic processes investigating the virtues, martyrdom or miracles of a servant of God in detail, the court must take care that the members of his religious congregation do not go astray in their evidence through mistaken loyalty. For obvious reasons the confessor, postulator, advocate, pro-curator and judges of the case are not allowed to give evidence.

(2) Experts are indispensable in the proof of miracles. They are generally selected by the tribunal inquiring into the miraculous events, but in the apostolic processes the congregation through the cardinal spokesman usually nominates the experts directly from the panel of doctors attached to the congregation, and they undertake to devote special study to the case.

There must be at least two experts, and as a general rule they carry out their examinations and write their reports independently, and are examined individually.

(3) As may be expected, this form of proof must also be surrounded by all the guarantees in documentary form that it is humanly possible to obtain, both as to their authenticity and to their probative value, taking into account the circumstances in which they first saw the light.

The documents which have a bearing on beatification causes are contemporary texts relating the facts under discussion. Later historical works have no value except in so far as they are derived from such texts. In addition it is essential that these documents really are what they purport to be, that is, that they are genuine. The authenticity of a text must, of course, be established by scientific historical methods.

In this field the Sacred Congregation of Rites has been supplemented in recent years by the addition of a "historical section" set up by Pius XI on February 6th, 1930, and designed to examine historical documents referring to ancient causes, whether they are tried by ordinary or extraordinary procedure. In these causes the congregation on January 4th, 1939, ordered the bishops—even before the diocesan or informative process is begun—to nominate a commission of three members, well versed in historical matters, of whom two must not belong to the religious congregation of the servant of God, to seek out all the relevant documents and report upon them to the diocesan court as witnesses *ex officio*. As we shall see later, when dealing with the miracles in the apostolic processes, a similar innovation has been introduced in the Sacred Congregation of Rites with the recent creation of a "special medical commission."

The diocesan or informative process to establish the servant of God's reputation for sanctity falls naturally into three smaller processes:

The process designed to collect the writings of the servant of God in order to pass judgment on his doctrine;

The informative process properly so called, the purpose of which is to establish the reputation for sanctity (*fama sanctitatis*) of the servant of God;

The process which aims to prove that the servant of God has never received any official cultus. In the course of this process the court must pay a special visit to the grave to see with their own eyes that there are no signs of official devotion there.

In this informative process the competent tribunal is that of the ordinary of the place where the servant of God died, and is presided over by the bishop or his delegate, who is present at each sitting together with the other members of the court.

Clearly the bishop has no power to pass judgment on the servant of God's reputation for sanctity. That is the prerogative of the Holy See. Hence every informative process must be sent to Rome as soon as it is completed, which is normally within two years after its inception.

The congregation carefully examines the informative process, beginning with a "revision of the writings." This is the first hurdle to be overcome and it is said, not without wit, that a servant of God who fails "in the written" has no chance.

Then comes the discussion of the informative process

proper. The sacred congregation must decide on the validity of the informative process. To this end it makes sure that all the rules of procedure have been meticulously observed, that all has been done according to the law, and that there is no obstacle to the "introduction of the cause at the Roman court," after having heard—or rather read, for all this is done in writing—the objections of the promoter of the faith. If the congregation sees fit to persevere with the cause it petitions the Pope to "sign the introduction of the cause." From that moment the process becomes "apostolic" and the bishop who was responsible for the informative process thereby loses all jurisdiction over the cause because the Holy See has "laid its hand upon it."

The apostolic process, as a rule, takes place at least fifty years after the death of the servant of God, although there are exceptions (like St Thérèse of the Child Jesus, St Maria Goretti and St Pius X) which go to prove the rule.

Rome, and Rome alone, can take the initiative in these processes, which are usually undertaken by the bishop of the place at her request. (This is called a "rogatory commission.") The bishop receives "remissorial letters" from the sacred congregation in which he is given instructions how to proceed, which must be carried out to the letter. A tribunal is set up, presided over by the bishop or his delegate assisted by four judges, by the sub-promoter of the faith and the notary. All these officials take an oath before the bishop at the session at which the court is constituted. This session is conducted with great solemnity in the bishop's chapel or other oratory. In principle every session of the apostolic process must be held in a sacred building, and at the end of each session the questionnaires sent by the Roman promoter of the faith together with the witnesses' replies must be sealed in an envelope which must not be opened outside the court—all under pain of nullity. Clearly no precaution is omitted to ensure the secrecy of questions and evidence.

We ought to add that before giving evidence the witnesses themselves must swear to speak the truth, and afterward swear to secrecy both about the questions put and the answers given, under threat of excommunication reserved to the Pope. The oath of secrecy expires when the probative phase of the apostolic process has been completed by the bishop's decree ordering the "publication of the process" and its transcription for dispatch to Rome.

The questionnaires deal with the theological, cardinal and moral virtues. As in the informative process, the witnesses must give an exact account of the sources of their information and state whether their evidence is based on personal experience or on what they have heard at such and such a time, in such and such circumstances . . .

At the end of the apostolic process (before its publication) comes the most moving movement of the whole affair, the "recognition of the body" of the servant of God. The bishop and full court, attended by the medical experts, proceed to the exhumation, opening of the coffin and description of the body of the servant of God in the state in which it is found. Thereafter the body is placed in a new coffin and generally transferred to a new resting place in a chapel or oratory, not, however, under an altar.

In the final session, which is as solemn as the first, the apostolic process, copied entirely by hand, is entrusted to a "courier" who takes an oath that he will faithfully hand over the sealed package to the sacred congregation. Generally this courier is none other than the vice-postulator of the cause, who may also fulfil his commission by giving it to the local apostolic nuncio or a diplomatic representative of the Holy See.

The sacred congregation—as in the informative process—first decides upon the procedural validity of the apostolic process, and then examines the main body of the process, the heroicity of the servant of God's virtues. This is undoubtedly the most formidable obstacle in the whole cause, and the servant of God must, through his advocate, overcome all the objections made by the "devil's advocate," the promoter of the faith. The sacred congregation, after three meetings called the "preliminary, preparatory and general congregations" (*congregatio antepreparatoria, preparatoria, generalis*), then pronounces judgment on the following question: Whether it is established that the servant of God practised the Christian virtues to a heroic degree? If the answer is in the affirmative, the congregation suggests that the Pope sign the decree of "heroicity of the virtues." From that moment the servant of God is called "Venerable."

The apostolic process on miracles is the decisive stage in the process of beatification or canonisation, for it embodies a sort of divine and tangible proof of sanctity.

As a general rule *two* miracles are required for beatification. The less conclusive the evidence for the virtues, the more are the miracles demanded by the Church. This is the idea behind the decree of the Sacred Congregation of Rites dated April 23rd, 1741, which requires two miracles for beatification if the witnesses to the heroicity of the virtues were eyewitnesses, and four if the evidence for heroicity or martyrdom was not derived from eyewitnesses. On July 17th, 1744, Benedict XIV somewhat modified this: provided eyewitnesses had given testimony to the virtues or martyrdom of the servant of God at the informative process, two miracles were sufficient even though at the apostolic process the witnesses had merely received their information from eyewitnesses. If, however, they had received it from others, at least three miracles were needed. These rules do not apply to martyrs.

In the case of martyrs, if the fact of martyrdom is clearly established, marvellous signs (what we have called "prodigies" above, p. 23) may suffice. By these are understood strange happenings, the miraculous nature of which is not subjected to any rigorous proof. These signs are discussed at the same time as the fact of martyrdom and do not usually involve the presence of experts. After it ha spassed its decree on the martyrdom, the congregation decides whether these signs are sufficient, whether their miraculous character must be looked into more closely or whether other miracles are required. On the other hand the decree on the martyrdom may simply dispense in the Pope's name from all this, as happened on March 25th, 1945, in the case of the young Italian virgin, Maria Goretti, whose martyrdom in 1902 had been adequately established by the evidence of eyewitnesses. This young martyr was canonised on June 25th, 1950.

In proof of the miracles two experts must be heard at the outset. If both agree in rejecting the miracle, no further steps are taken.

When it is a question of deciding upon the cure of a disease, as in the majority of cases, the experts must have a certain standing in medicine or surgery; indeed, if at all possible, care is taken to select specialists well known for their skill in diagnosis and treatment of that particular disease. The experts' reports, concisely worded and clearly supported by arguments, must reply to the following queries:

If a cure is alleged, can the person in whose favour it is claimed be held as truly cured?

Can the fact put forward as miraculous be explained by the laws of nature or not?

In his masterly treatise "On the Beatification and Canonisation of Servants of God" Benedict XIV lists the seven characteristics which stamp a cure as miraculous. He writes:

"Several conditions must be fulfilled *simultaneously* before the cure of a disease or infirmity can be reckoned as miraculous:

"1. The disease must be serious and impossible, or at least very difficult, to cure;

"2. The disease must not have reached a stage at which it was liable to disappear shortly of its own accord;

"3. No medical treatment must have been applied, or if it were, it must have certainly been ineffectual;

"4. The cure must be sudden, instantaneous;

"5. The cure must be complete;

"6. It must not be preceded by any crisis due to natural causes at the expected time; otherwise the cure, far from being miraculous, must be considered either wholly or partially as natural;

"7. Finally, there must be no relapse into the same disease after the cure."

There can, of course, be true miracles which do not fulfil one or other of these conditions. But while the Church does not deny the possibility of less "complete" miracles, it must be emphasised that she refuses to accept them officially, so insistent is she on signs which are exact, easily recognisable and leaving no loophole for error.

Some doctors are surprised to learn how much the Church demands before acknowledging an extraordinary cure as miraculous. The present writer, who took part in a court of inquiry into an alleged miraculous cure, heard a medical witness, no great believer, pass this delightful remark: "How is it that I, who am not very strong in faith nor in the practice of my religion, am sure there is a miracle in this case, whereas you Church judges are harder to convince than I?"

Others may think that some of Benedict XIV's rules— now 200 years old—are ripe for revision. This suggestion cannot be ruled out of court *a priori* and it casts no aspersion whatever either on Benedict XIV or on the Sacred Congregation of Rites. It is right and proper that Catholic doctors of repute should make themselves heard by the authorities in Rome, setting forth their views with all the necessary details and taking into account the most recent progress made in medicine and surgery in this century of scientific discovery.

In any event the sacred congregation, as it has already done in another field in setting up a "historical section," has every intention of using specialist knowledge in the medical field as well. It has in fact recently established an experimental college of doctors to discuss the miracles adduced in beatification and canonisation causes. This commission or college, which meets after two or three doctors have made a preliminary survey of the case, comprises seven or eight members. It has been in operation since 1949 and in practice its rôle is that of the "antepreparatory" congregation. From the medical point of view its verdict is final. It goes without saying that the latest developments in medicine are used. It is an invariable rule that cures of nervous disorders are not regarded by the sacred congregation as miraculous, and this applies in general to cures worked in hypersensitive cases whose emotional nature is such as might produce "nervous discharges" capable of affecting their power of moving, for example.

The sittings devoted to the examination of the miracles are always three in number. The usual number of miracles to be discussed in the preliminary and preparatory sessions is two; but if there are more, a dispensation may be given to enable them to be taken together. That is what happened in the case of the three miracles attributed to Claude de la Colombière, which were discussed in the preliminary session on May 1st, 1928, and in the preparatory session on January 29th, 1929.[3]

The question to be answered at these meetings is worded thus: Whether it is certain that there are miracles in the case and have they the required effect?

In the preliminary session the agenda (*positio*) contains: a digest compiled by the advocate, a summary of the evidence given by the witnesses, the two reports of the experts on each miracle, the objections of the promoter-general of the faith and the advocate's replies.

Where miraculous cures are under review the digest serves to describe the sick persons, the progress of their disease and the circumstances in which they came to invoke the servant of God. The summary reproduces the eyewitnesses' accounts of the disease and its cure and the prayers used in asking the servant of God for a cure. If the two experts agree in accepting the miracle as certain, the promoter's objections may cast doubt on the connection between it and the servant of God's intercession. In this way a miracle which took place at Lourdes was nevertheless retained for the canonisation of St Joan of Arc— the circumstances in which the miracle was worked proved too strong for the promoter of the faith's objections and it was definitely ascribed to St Joan.

The preparatory session is devoted to an examination of the conclusions reached in the previous session regarding the experts' reports, after a third and even a fourth expert has been called in to make a supplementary report confirming, disagreeing with or deciding between the original experts. The members of this preparatory congregation occasionally find themselves cast in the ticklish rôle of a judge faced with contradictory expert opinions. In that case the cardinals demand fresh information before coming to any conclusion.

A general congregation is held in the presence of the Pope and consists in an outline of the whole cause since the degree on the virtues. The final objections of the promoter of the faith are heard, together with the advocate's refutation. But in this session the Pope does not immediately pronounce judgment on the miracles themselves. The decree of approbation of the miracles is only published in the official organ of the Holy See (*Acta Apostolicae Sedis*) after an interval of several days. Thus the decree approving the miracles of St John Bosco was promulgated fourteen days after the general congregation.[4]

After the decree of approbation of the miracles has been passed, a new discussion must take place before the Holy Father on the following point: Whether it is now safe (*tuto*) to proceed to the beatification of the servant of God? It is the Pope himself who, after hearing the opinions of the consultors and cardinals, decides this issue and causes the decree *De Tuto* to be drawn up and promulgated. Nothing now remains but to fix the date of the beatification ceremony. This consists essentially in the reading of the brief of beatification in St Peter's in the presence of the cardinals of the Sacred Congregation of Rites, of the cardinal archpriest and clergy of the Vatican Basilica, the postulator, all those concerned in the process, the family of the new *beatus*, and the crowds of the faithful who always attend these functions.

As soon as the brief has been read—and this, we repeat, is the official proclamation of the beatification—the "Te Deum" is intoned by the officiating prelate, and at the same moment the picture of the beatus is unveiled above the "Chair of St Peter" in the magnificent décor of Bernini's "Gloria". A solemn Mass is then offered in honour of the *beatus*. In the evening the Pope comes down to St Peter's to venerate the relics of the *beatus* amid the enthusiasm of the crowd.

Before canonisation two more miracles (three, if the beatification was only equivalent), which took place after beatification, must be approved. The apostolic processes on the miracles are conducted in the same way as in the beatification process. The liturgical ceremony of canonisation is carried out with greater solemnity than that of beatification, and its essential feature is the proclamation of canonization read by the Pope himself, the wording of which dates from the year 1313:

G

"In honour of the holy and undivided Trinity, for the exaltation of the Catholic faith and the increase of the Christian religion, by the authority of Our Lord Jesus Christ, of the blessed apostles Peter and Paul and our own, after mature deliberation and having frequently implored the divine aid, in accordance with the desires of our venerable brethren the cardinals, patriarchs, archbishops and bishops assembled in this city, we declare and define that N. is a saint, and we inscribe him in the catalogue of the saints, and order that his memory shall be kept with piety and devotion on such and such a date, in the ranks of the martyrs (confessors, virgins . . .). In the name of the Father and of the Son and of the Holy Ghost. Amen."

The Papal Mass is then celebrated in this unique setting, which seems to foreshadow the heavenly Jerusalem.

To illustrate what has been said we can do no better than add a description of the miracles approved for the recent canonizations of St Grignion de Montfort and St Jeanne de Lestonnac. No more fitting means could be found to display the wisdom and prudence with which the judgments of the Church regarding the honour paid to her saints are inspired.

CHAPTER V

CANONISATION MIRACLES[1]

Miracles admitted by the Sacred Congregation of Rites for the Canonisation of St Louis-Marie Grignion de Montfort (1947)

CURE OF SISTER GERARD OF CALVARY (1927)
(Visceral tuberculosis with fistulae)

Sister Gerard of Calvary was suffering from tuberculosis of both lungs and ulcerated tuberculosis of the pelvic peritoneum, with two fistulae discharging purulent matter. This combination of diseases had brought her to the point of death and the Sacrament of Extreme Unction had been administered. There was no possible remedy, so fervent prayers were addressed to Blessed Louis-Marie to intercede on her behalf.

The patient was visited by her doctor in the morning of April 8th, 1927. He has since declared on oath that he found her in a dying condition. That afternoon she was instantaneously cured. Not only was she able to resume her normal activities, but within two days some of the heaviest work fell to her lot. She has since continued to enjoy better health than before her illness.

The miraculous character of the cure was admitted, not only by the three experts chosen by the sacred congregation, but also by her own doctor, who, though not a Catholic, made a clear statement to that effect under oath.

CURE OF SISTER MARIE-THÉRÈSE LESAGE (1934)
(Tuberculous meningitis)

There is no doubt that Sister Marie-Thérèse Lesage was predisposed to tuberculosis, not only because the disease was common in her family, but also because she had herself suffered from it in childhood. In June, 1934, she contracted tuberculous meningitis. Three doctors were consulted and each unhesitatingly gave the same diagnosis; later, the three experts appointed by the sacred congregation could only confirm it. All agreed that the disease was certainly fatal.[2] Since there was no hope of a natural recovery, fervent prayers were said that God might, through the intercession of Blessed Louis-Marie, be pleased to restore the sick nun to health.

This hope was not disappointed. In the evening of July 24th, feast of St John the Baptist, the patient suddenly recovered the power of speech and showed herself full of energy and vitality. Two days later she felt perfectly cured. According to the experts the cure was still maintained in November of the following year.

The three doctors consulted, together with the three experts designated by the sacred congregation, were unanimous in declaring that there had been a miraculous intervention of God.

Canonical processes were introduced by the Bishops of Portsmouth and Luçon with a view to the recognition of these cures as miraculous, and their validity was accepted by the Sacred Congregation of Rites on February 1st, 1939.

Miracles admitted for the Canonisation of St Jeanne de Lestonnac (1949)

CURE OF MOTHER ADELA PALOMBO (1941)

(Mastoiditis with intracranial complications)

On October 24th, 1935, a young Italian woman, Mother Palombo, arrived at Tournemire, Southern France, in a very poor state of health. Her physical development had been retarded by a serious accident in her youth. In addition one of her ears troubled her, and a Roman specialist had prescribed treatment, hinting at the necessity of a surgical operation. However, Mother Palombo bore her affliction with patience for some years, and continued to do good work. Because of her skill in that line she was in charge of the housekeeping course.

Nevertheless there is a limit to human resistance to disease, whatever the strength of the will. Thus, shortly before the declaration of war the pain in her head and ear became so violent that the doctor attached to the house, Doctor Veyrac of Roquefort, suggested that she should be examined by a specialist. By this time hostilities had broken out, the local specialist was called up and Mother Palombo had to be taken to Albi to Doctor Bonpunt, an ear, nose and throat specialist, who considered the case very serious and decided that an immediate operation was necessary.

On December 9th, 1939, Mother Palombo underwent an operation for the draining of the mastoid antrum, lasting five hours. She was looked after by the doctor and sisters of the Boutge Clinic, Albi. She gradually recovered, but the wound did not cicatrise until the following June. She had, however, left the clinic in April and stayed at the Notre Dame Convent in Albi. Each time the dressing was renewed she experienced severe pain in spite of Dr Bonpunt's precautions.

In consequence Mother Palombo only returned to Tournemire in June, 1940. She looked well enough, her appetite was good and she was once more able to take up her ordinary work, although the headaches had never completely disappeared. In August attacks of giddiness and nausea developed and in September Mother Palombo had to go back to Albi for examination. Dr Bonpunt found nothing abnormal and prescribed a course of tonics. Unfortunately the patient's condition was becoming worse, and Dr Veyrac, when on leave from the army, observed that she was much thinner and so weak that she often had to stay in bed.

When the doctor observed her continual vomiting attacks he suspected an abscess on the brain and insisted on another visit to the specialist. The hard winter and the wartime dislocation of communications made it impossible to visit Albi until March 1941. She was then so ill that her fellow travellers were full of pity for her, convinced that she would die on the way.

Mother Palombo was put under observation once more in the Boutge Clinic, but went from bad to worse, and Doctor Ducoudray, head of the Bon Sauveur Hospital, who was called into consultation, did all he could to relieve her, but in vain. A second operation was unavoidable. The patient absolutely refused. She was then in full possession of her faculties and all she wanted was to return to Tournemire to die.

On her return the ambulance was met by the assembled religious, who had the strong impression that it would not be long before Mother Palombo was called to God. She received

Extreme Unction and it was decided to make a novena to Blessed Jeanne de Lestonnac. The sick nun joined in with great fervour, but was clearly sinking fast.

On May 1st, just as the community was in the chapel finishing the prayers for the last day of the novena, Mother Palombo felt a hand rest lightly on the left side of her head and heard the words: "Rise up. You are cured." This she told to an Italian nun who came to see if she needed anything and who immediately went to tell the mother superior. The superior at once went to the sickroom and found Mother Palombo sitting up in bed, radiant with joy.

She got up and dressed without assistance and then went to the chapel. Today Mother Palombo is perfectly cured, takes her full share in the life of the community and has never been so well.

The apostolic process set up to examine this cure took place in July, 1942, at Tournemire. On this occasion Professor Sympa, medical expert attached to the Sacred Congregation of Rites, came specially from Rome.

The nun told the story of her cure in the following terms:

"I left the clinic on April 20th and returned to Tournemire by ambulance. When I arrived I was at the end of my tether; I thought I was going to die. I was anointed on April 22nd, and on the 23rd the novena to Blessed Jeanne was started. The first thing I did was to stop taking any medicine, with the exception of a thread from material which had touched our Blessed Mother's bones. This I did every day. During the novena the pain was worse than ever—the fever increased and the vomiting hardly stopped. The worst time was the ninth day. At four o'clock in the morning I was in terrible pain and thought my last hour had come because my heart began to falter from time to time so that I could not breathe. The infirmarian was very worried. . . . Suddenly I felt quite drowsy, and a hand was laid lightly upon my head, while I heard a clear voice say to me: 'Rise up, you are cured.' I turned round quickly to see who was there—and although the slightest movement had caused me to vomit before, nothing happened this time—but I saw nobody. I was afraid and began to tremble. I hid my head under the bedclothes, saying: 'My God, what is it? What is happening?' Fortunately the assistant infirmarian had asked permission to come up during the meal to see how I was and if I needed anything, for she had left me in great pain when she had gone to breakfast. She was amazed to find me trembling like a leaf. I said: 'I want to get up. I'm cured,' and told her what had happened. She cried out, 'It's a miracle!' and rushed to fetch the reverend mother provincial, who came at once and told me to get up.

"My head felt quite all right. I dressed myself and we went down to the choir, knelt before the statue of our Blessed Mother and poured out our thanks. Then I went to the community room where the novices and nuns were gathered in great excitement, and they all embraced me affectionately. At half past three I went to solemn Benediction of the Blessed Sacrament, and spent the whole time on my knees without feeling tired. At the end we sang a hymn in praise of our holy foundress. And now, what can I say about myself? I eat well— on the very evening of the cure I ate a good tea and had the same supper as the others. My head is very well, better than it has been for several years. The community doctor saw me and could only say: 'It's a miracle.' He told me he had expected either a miracle or death.

(Signed) Adela Palombo, Fille de Notre Dame."

Cure of Sister Maria del Carmen Gay (1920)
(Cancer of the intestine)

In 1920 Sister Maria, a nun in the community of Callella, Spain, was suffering from cancer of the intestine, the first symptoms of which had appeared six years before.[3] Early in 1920 the pain began to increase in intensity. She received the last Sacraments in August, but dragged on with many ups and downs until November, when she took a turn for the worse. By now the pain was well nigh unbearable, and she was almost paralysed down one side. In the morning of November 5th the community began a novena to their foundress, Blessed Jeanne de Lestonnac, to pray for Sister Maria's recovery. During the novena, since the doctors had said there was no remedy for her disease, no medicines were used except for some injections of camphorated oil to relieve the pain. On November 11th, the sixth day of the novena, she received Holy Communion at 6.15 a.m. While she was making her thanksgiving she dozed off for some minutes and awoke to find that disease, pain, paralysis had all vanished. . . . She got up, realised she was cured, dressed without difficulty and left her room. We may imagine the infirmarian's surprise to find her patient, not in bed where she had left her, incapable of standing erect and requiring several nuns to lift her, but walking in the corridor.

Since that memorable day Sister Maria has shared to the full in the life of the community and has resumed her former duties as cobbler, working hard without any trace of her trouble.

Application was made to the sacred congregation and the order was given to conduct an inquiry into the cure. Doctor Salvattori, medical expert to the sacred congregation, came from Rome for that purpose. The ecclesiastical court sat morning and evening for eleven days, examining the sister herself, the witnesses, and the doctors who had treated her during her illness. The court brought in two other doctors unknown to the nun, and these gave their opinions after a very careful examination.

The process was transferred to Rome in May, 1922. The preparatory work continued until January 4th, 1924, when the process set up in Gerona and Callella was approved by the sacred congregation. There were, however, difficulties to be overcome, and in particular one expression in the translation of the documents failed to satisfy the doctors. It was therefore necessary to refer the case back to Gerona, and it was not until January, 1928, that the Roman doctors unanimously accepted the cure. On August 8th, 1928, the miracle was finally approved by the sacred congregation.

CHAPTER VI

THE LOURDES MEDICAL BUREAU

Origin and Early Cures

MGR Billère set up the medical bureau officially in 1884,[1] and put it under the direction of Dr de Saint-Maclou. Prior to that time, however, there had existed an official body of a kind which supervised the cures then taking place.

So close has been the relationship between the events at Lourdes and the medical profession's supervisory task, so fundamental the activity of medical men, that one might almost suggest that Our Lady had deliberately brought about this state of affairs and had specifically willed that medical supervision should be a feature of her activity. This intervention of the human in the supernatural, this background of natural scientific activity to the miraculous, continues to this day, its influence becoming steadily more widespread.

From the beginning of the apparitions doctors were about, and the spirit of medical inquiry can be seen in the questing personality of Dr Dozous. He was sceptical at first, but became the careful witness of the first cures and can be regarded as the forerunner of the Bureau of Medical Records.

CURE OF PIERRE BOURIETTE (1858)
(*Traumatic blindness*)

Pierre Bouriette was a quarry worker on the Pic du Jer. It was his job to set off the blasting charges which produced stones for the quarry men.

Twenty years before the apparitions, in 1838, his right eye had been injured by an explosion which had damaged it. Since that date he could only just see with it because of corneal scarring.

One day he came to Dr Dozous and stated that he understood "Bernadette's water cured people."

He could hardly have said this, had it not already been spread abroad that miraculous cures had occurred in Lourdes almost immediately after the water had started to flow under Bernadette's groping fingers.

Dr Dozous was probably aware of this and his earliest reaction to the tale of cures may well have been simply mercenary in view of the possibility of exploiting commercially the thermal qualities of the spring.

However, hearing that the waters were being credited with supernatural powers, he was thrown on the defensive; his reply to Bouriette was, "You can go to Bernadette's spring if you like. Come back cured and I'll believe in its powers."

These bold words can still be heard, but those who speak them do not act up to them, preferring, when faced with a cure, to fall back on somebody's mistaken diagnosis rather than admit that there exists an Intelligence greater than ours, transcendental, infinite, Creator and Organiser of the universe, which, having made all the laws of nature, retains the right and power to alter them, not as we wish, but as It wills; that is, retains the right to perform a miracle.[2]

Three days after his interview with Dr Dozous, Bouriette washed his blind eye in the still muddy spring water. He did not really have much faith in the water's powers; curiosity rather than hope was the driving force behind his action. (The majority of visitors to Lourdes still go there in this frame of mind.)

He was quite taken aback when he realised that, when he had washed his eye, he could see with both of them. It might be thought that his immediate reaction would have been to thank the Lady of the Apparitions, or Bernadette, who happened to be there at the time. He actually did what not a few still do, he rushed to the physician to have his cure properly verified. As soon as Bouriette saw the doctor he shouted that he was cured. Dr Dozous, who had quite forgotten the talk some days before, said, "My dear man, that isn't possible—the stuff I gave you can't cure you—the drops are simply to prevent you feeling pain and to avoid infection

developing in the other eye." "But it's not you who's cured
me, doctor—it's Bernadette's water." "I can't accept that,"
said Dr Dozous and, turning his back on Bouriette's now
healthy eye, he wrote on a sheet of paper a technical phrase
that Bouriette could neither know nor invent. "Bouriette
suffers from an incurable amaurosis. He cannot see; he never
will." Covering Bouriette's healthy eye with his hand, he
asked him to read what he had written. This Bouriette did.
"I could hardly have been more shattered if a thunderbolt
had fallen at my feet," Dr Dozous states in his account of the
incident.

Here, then, was the first medical recording of a miraculous
cure in Lourdes; and the first crack in Dr Dozous' façade of
philosophic scientific scepticism.

Being a conscientious doctor and loyal natural scientist, he
promptly set about observing the grotto at Massabielle with
the help of his only available measuring instrument—a watch.
As a result he witnessed the second historically recorded cure—
that of Louis-Justin Bouhohorts.

CURE OF LOUIS BOUHOHORTS (1858)
(*Osteomalacia and febrile wasting*)

Louis Bouhohorts was eighteen months old. He lay quite
still in his cot, for he had not moved since birth. He suffered
from a syndrome characterised by fragility of his bones—then
given the name osteomalacia. He never had moved, nor sat,
nor stood up—nor, obviously, had he ever walked.

In addition to this he suffered from a febrile, wasting disorder which had at that time brought him to death's door. As
he lay *in extremis* in his cot his father remarked to his mother,
still stubbornly nursing him, "Let him be; it's obvious he's
nearly dead." At which he left to fetch a neighbour to sew his
shroud—who soon arrived with the necessary material. But
his mother would have none of it—a mother's heart may go
on hoping so long as to move God's heart.

She snatched the child from his cot and wrapped him
hurriedly in the first thing that came to hand—a kitchen
cloth. Running to the grotto, she covered the last fifty yards
on her knees. (This part was then rough and stony, unlike
the smooth modern pathways.) Making her way through

about forty curious people standing at the foot of the grotto, she arrived to find Bernadette praying and Dr Dozous awaiting events, watch in hand.

There was a small pool, roughly five feet by two, dug by quarry workers of the Pic du Jer in thanksgiving for their fellow worker Bouriette's cure. Into this icy water (48°F) she plunged young Louis-Justin to his neck. She kept him there for fifteen and a half minutes (timed by Dr Dozous). When she took him out he was stiff and blue, which was hardly to be wondered at.

Perhaps the reader has not been bathed in the baths at Lourdes. Dr Leuret stayed in for fifteen seconds—the usual time. "I must confess that I did this neither in a spirit of faith nor of penance, but from a professional point of view as, being responsible for the distribution of bathing cards, I felt it incumbent on me to know to what I was subjecting all sorts of sick—bedridden and infected cases, cardiac cases, lung cases, even the dying."

The experience can only be described as extremely unpleasant. (The translators can confirm this statement.) One is plunged suddenly and without regard into icy water. One is seized by a sense of thoracic constriction and strangulation so acute that were it not for the presence of stretcher-bearers whose task is to recite the prescribed prayers, no word of the subject's would reach Our Lady. It is undoubtedly the greatest and most lasting of miracles in the baths at Lourdes that no sick person, however seriously ill, suffers from the immersion, nor does his or her illness get worse.

Louis-Justin Bouhohorts was taken out of the water cold and blue. His mother, rather ashamed of what she had been doing, wrapped him, still stiff, in his kitchen cloth, took him into her arms, returned home and put him in his cot.

When his father saw him in this condition he felt no anger but simply said to his wife, "Well, you should be happy anyway, you've managed to kill him off." He turned away with tears in his eyes while the child's mother remained in prayer beside the cot. After some moments she tugged at her husband's coat. "Look—he's breathing." Which, in fact, he was. He fell asleep now and spent a quiet night. He woke gurgling next morning and took his breakfast—this, despite his age, at his mother's breast. According to her he had a good meal. She put him back in his cot and went into the next room to do her household chores. Leaving him alone did not worry her—he had never moved.

A little later she heard behind her the patter of feet. On looking around there was Louis-Justin—cured of all his sufferings, the osteomalacia, the wasting illness which had almost carried him off. Furthermore, he could walk—without having learned to walk.[3]

This unusual story, whose genuineness cannot be doubted, stultifies the major objection that materialist natural scientists of the nineteenth century put forward so confidently—faith heals. Dr Leuret himself heard his teacher, Dr Pitres, say, when he knew that he was off to Lourdes. "Well, I've no doubt you'll see plenty of cases of autosuggestion there, with flowers, wreaths, incense and collective prayers thrown in!"

There were none of these things for Louis-Justin Bouhohorts—no flowers, chants, prayers or incense. Just a few rather sceptical curiosity-seekers and an observant but cautious doctor. In any case, the child was only eighteen months old. It seems unlikely that a child of that age could make an act of faith, or be susceptible to this type of suggestion, but there undoubtedly is a healing faith, one which asks and prays,[4] a faith which springs from those who forget themselves and ask for the healing of their unhappy brethren. This is the faith of the sick, of their stretcher-bearers, of those, ever present, who pray night and day at Our Lady's feet.

Louis-Justin Bouhohorts' cure convinced Dr Dozous, first medical witness of the events at Massabielle and initiator of the medical supervision carried out at Lourdes.

THE BUREAU OF MEDICAL RECORDS

Quite apart from the early proofs of Our Lady's goodness, which throw so much light on Bernadette's honesty and sincerity, these have been vouched for by a

commission of three psychiatrists, Drs Balancie, La-
crampe and Peyrus, appointed by Baron Massy, prefect
of the department, to investigate her mental state. We
may discern in this a confirmation of our suggestion that
Our Lady desires this sort of medical supervision, which
contributes so much to our knowledge, for these gentlemen
were given clear indications that they were to declare
Bernadette mentally defective and dangerous to public
order; they were to sign the necessary documents com-
mitting her to a mental home without further ado.

However, the three doctors were men of independence
and spirit, thoroughly courageous in professional matters.
They questioned and examined Bernadette at length and
then refused to submit to the prefect's suggestion. They
stated quite clearly in their report that Bernadette was
sane in mind, not hallucinated and that if she had
manifested "a state of ecstasy" there was in her no
suspicion of lying nor of mental instability which might
render her a menace to the peace of the realm, and they
formally concluded that she should be set at liberty.

It might be suggested that had these three men not
been possessed of a sense of public duty, had they weakly
fallen in with the suggestion (almost an order) made to
them, had they hesitated or evaded the issue, the Lourdes
story would in all probability have ended there and then.
The whole matter would have been forgotten and nothing
further would have happened. We should have been
deprived for more than ninety years of the source of
consolation to be found in this holy place at Lourdes.

The first cures, combined with Dr Dozous' medical
supervision and the expert psychiatric examination of
Bernadette, constitute the earliest signs of medical activity
concerned with the events at Lourdes and therefore of
the Lourdes Medical Bureau.

In 1885 a clinic was organised in a wooden hut not far
from the baths.

From then onward all investigations into the cures

were undertaken in these rather primitive surroundings by Dr de Saint-Maclou. With the help of a nun or priest who acted as secretary and kept the registers (which still exist) Dr de Saint-Maclou undertook the responsibility of scientific investigation and of drawing conclusions.

Dr Boissarie succeeded Dr de Saint-Maclou in 1892. Five hundred medical men visited the Bureau of Medical Records in the pilgrimage season of that year—from July to October. Many a bridge was crossed and many a prejudice overcome. At the present time between fifteen hundred and two thousand doctors come every year to the medical bureau, not merely as visitors, but to have a share in its work.

For thirty years Dr Boissarie presided over the Bureau of Medical Records with that fine clinical spirit and respect for truth and objective fact which are an example to the medical scientists today.

Dr Boissarie examined cases of alleged miraculous cures with the greatest care. The case notes of the examining doctors were subjected to the most rigorous scrutiny; frauds (present then as now) were unmasked and thrown out with what amounted almost to violence.

When this great man (whom some hope to see beatified) died in 1917 he was succeeded by two physicians worthy of him. Dr le Bec, master general of the Guild of St Luke, surgeon to St Joseph's Hospital in Paris, was made titular head of the Bureau of Medical Records. His university and hospital work, however, did not allow him to carry out his task in more than an honorary capacity, so that the guardian of the grotto (the Lourdes title of the bishops of Tarbes) appointed a resident vice-president, Dr Marchand.

Meanwhile the earlier bureau had been transferred from its wooden hut to the rooms under the ramp leading up over the Rosary Church, beneath the statue of St Luke, where it remained till 1947.

Since then others have succeeded to this enviable post.

Dr Abadie-Bayro put forward a plan, which he had fostered for thirty-odd years, for the reorganisation and functioning of the medical bureau. A considerable part of the present set-up has been based on these plans. Next came Dr Vallet,[5] who was in charge for twenty-five years and to whom belongs the credit for the foundation of the International Medical Association of Lourdes. This is the strong and effective pillar which supports the whole moral and material framework of the medical bureau.

PRESENT MEDICAL ORGANISATION

In 1947, after Dr Vallet's voluntary retirement, the new Bishop of Lourdes, Mgr Théas, decided to reorganise the Lourdes Medical Bureau and the whole of its scientific structure.

He first established a commission of inquiry into the medical organisation of the bureau. This assembly's task was to suggest such changes in scientific method in practice and in financial matters as might have a bearing on the bureau's activity. The commission was made up of eighteen doctors and four priests under the chairmanship of Mgr Théas.

This commission considered it essential to set up a scientific body at Lourdes of such a nature that no doubt could be cast upon the objectivity of investigations undertaken there.

The task of the medical bureau is to investigate, impartially and objectively, the numerous alleged miracles which occur at Lourdes throughout the pilgrimage period. Its task is no longer to decide on the miraculous nature of the cures whose genuineness it records. The medical bureau has, of course, the right to pronounce upon the authenticity of the phenomena it investigates, but is not called upon to determine whether they are miraculous or not. This decision lies with bodies properly set up by the Church, e.g. diocesan canonical commissions, appointed by the bishop under whose ecclesiastical jurisdiction the cured person lives. There has been for some time past a great deal of unfortunate misunderstanding about this matter by the ever credulous public.

The medical bureau does not record miracles; it simply records facts. Its task is not to determine whether these are miraculous.

It must be repeated that this question concerning the miraculous nature of a cure rests with the Church. This alone justifies the silence maintained by the Lourdes Medical Bureau. Surprise is often expressed that it does not rush into print after recording the phenomena. As long as theological confirmation of the facts is not forthcoming the bureau has no right to talk about a miracle in doctrine or in fact.

In order to give complete reliability to these pronouncements on questions of scientific fact, Mgr Théas set up a National Medical Commission attached to the Medical Bureau of Lourdes which examines scientifically the case notes of cures submitted to it by the Lourdes bureau. It must be understood that its task is purely technical. The commission's object is to deliver judgment on documents forwarded to it by the Lourdes bureau; it is not empowered to receive them directly. Nor can it be considered as a judicial body with superior status to that of the medical bureau. On the other hand, the bureau cannot pass on to the canonical commissions documents which have not yet satisfied the National Medical Commission.

The medical commission is made up of the following members:[6]

Dr Auvigne, director of the medical school, Nantes.

Dr R. Biot, Lyons.

Dr L. Cornet, Pau.

Dr P. Delore, assistant professor and physician to the Lyons hospitals.

Dr P. Giraud, professor in the medical faculty, physician to the Marseilles hospitals.

H

Dr H. Grenet, hon. physician to the Paris hospitals, president of the Medical Society of St Luke.

Dr G. Huc, surgeon to St Joseph's Hospital, Paris, associate member of the Academy of Surgery.

Canon Lancrenon, doctor of medicine.

Dr L. Langeron, professor in the medical faculty (free) of Lille, late physician to the Lyons hospitals.

Dr J. Lhermitte, assistant professor, member of the Academy of Medicine.

Dr P. Mauriac, dean of the Faculty of Medicine, physician to the Bordeaux hospitals, corresponding member of the Academy of Medicine.

Dr P. Merigot de Treigny, physician to St Joseph's Hospital, Paris.

Dr L. Michon, surgeon to the Paris hospitals, member of the Academy of Surgery.

Dr P. Sendrail, associate professor in the medical faculty, Toulouse.

This reorganisation involved many changes. A new site became necessary in view of the large attendance of pilgrims, sick and doctors. The existing bureau, under the ramp of the Rosary Church, had been set up when only 150,000 pilgrims and 1,500 sick came annually to Lourdes.

In contrast, in 1947, 750 doctors came; in 1948, 999; in 1950, 1,200. In 1948 Lourdes dealt with 2,000,000 pilgrims and 15,800 sick; in 1949 rather more than 3,000,000 pilgrims and more than 20,000 sick.

In the space then available little could be done. There was one room where all the activities of the medical staff took place: examination of the sick, medical conferences and, when the necessity arose, announcement of the findings of investigations. There were no facilities for technical investigation, no proper examination couch, and when a patient was to be examined it was necessary to stretch him out on the table at which the secretary was writing and on which the case notes were piled. No facilities for a reliable scientific examination existed either, no X-ray apparatus, only the simplest ausculatory equipment. Such a state of affairs could not be considered satisfactory in view of the widening scope of the medical bureau. It is clear, however, that no reflection is thereby cast on Drs Boissarie, Marchand, Cox, Abadie-Bayro, Vallet, who, with the limited means at their disposal, produced those critical observations of sick persons which have contributed so largely to the medical bureau's reputation.

It had become essential to enlarge the buildings in which medical work was carried out and to improve the technical equipment. This was the end which Mgr Théas had in view and which he has fully achieved. The old site of the medical bureau has been retained and altered.

The old examination and assembly room has been divided up so that it is now made up of two small, clean and comfortable rooms. Here two doctors can stay without charge and act as day and night duty medical officers dealing with accidents and incidents which occur in the domain of the grotto.[7] Next door is a small study and writing room where the medical officers can work. There are the usual modern conveniences.

The old museum is used as a small first-aid post. The museum itself consists of a lay-out of photographic posi- tives on glass, illuminated from behind.

The two small remaining rooms have been converted into a secretariat where the documents and case notes are filed. These can be referred to, whether the case has been retained as miraculous or not, by simply giving the secretary the name and year of the required case.

THE BUREAU OF SCIENTIFIC STUDIES

In view of the above state of affairs the rooms set aside for the examination of patients had to be moved else- where. Mgr Théas provided a large building made up of ten rooms, some large, some small. They are well ventilated, well lighted and sensibly laid out. In these rooms are carried out all clinical examinations of the sick. These apartments make up the Bureau of Scientific Studies. We shall justify this description farther on.

The main door is on the ground floor of the Hospitalité Building,[8] behind the pilgrims' shelter. It faces east, looking out over the underground basilica, and is approached by a path leading from a small esplanade where pilgrims may rest on the benches.

Inside the main door is the waiting room, supplied with seating arrangements for the sick. A nurse takes their names and addresses and that of their own doctor and directs them to the rooms where they are to be examined.

This practice makes it possible to contact the medical attendant, who is notified whenever any incident concerning his patient occurs during the pilgrimage. In this way the patient's personal doctor, irrespective of his attitude to the phenomena of Lourdes, is made aware of the existence of a technical body at Lourdes, and he can but reply to the letter which is sent to him. By these means he is brought into relationship with the Bureau of Scientific Studies.

The book of visiting doctors is also in the waiting room. In this they register their name, address, medical faculty, qualifications and speciality. The great increase in medical visitors which has already been recorded is a source of great joy to the president of the bureau. In the past few years have come unbelievers, agnostics, Protestants, Freemasons, atheists, Jews, Buddhists, Moslems, followers of Confucius, orthodox Greeks, etc., etc. Some have come openly hostile, others have gone with their original ideas disturbed; all have left honestly convinced of the care with which the medical examinations are carried out at the medical bureau. They are usually impressed by the sincerity of those working there, and (as several have admitted) this turns their minds to the question of the reality of supernatural phenomena.

It is worth repeating that the medical bureau is not a body acting behind closed doors. A papal passport is not necessary to attend its activities. The Lourdes Medical Bureau is, first and foremost, a scientific body where any medical man of whatever race, creed, colour or philosophy may come. He is not asked what he thinks, but simply if he is a doctor.[9] (Frauds have occasionally gained admittance.) Once inside, he has the right to read and see everything and to express his views. This fact is a guarantee of the value of the medical investigations undertaken in the bureau, for if only convinced Catholics signed the case notes they might be suspect. This suspicion can be reasonably excluded when non-believers are also signatories to these documents.

It is important to insist that one objection so often raised, namely that mistakes in diagnosis can account for alleged miracles, is untenable. Of course, every doctor has made mistakes. But is it likely that sixty or seventy doctors will all make the same mistake? There will surely always be one to show his colleagues where they are wrong. On October 15th, 1949, the 25,000th doctor was registered. Among this great number are found men whose competence is undeniable. In that same year the bureau had the benefit of the presence and opinion of forty-seven professors in medical faculties, both French and foreign. It has been visited by leaders of the profession from London, Glasgow, Dublin, Louvain, Liège, Padua, Geneva, Lyons, Paris, Lille, etc. These have included 150 surgeons to the hospitals of the major French cities; large numbers of all kinds of specialists, thirty-five neuropsychiatrists—an important fact as many still persist in their belief that only neuropaths are cured here —about forty chest physicians (tuberculosis specialists), as many ophthalmologists, dermatologists and otologists. Even more pædiatricians have attended—another particularly valuable fact in view of the many children cured at Lourdes.

In addition to all these, there have come to Lourdes many general practitioners from town and country with the wide experience and a common sense acquired by those who live continually amid the sick, often making important decisions without other opinion or help.

The waiting room contains a weighing machine and equipment for recording heights. These are necessary in view of the fact that patients often claim remarkable weight increases over a few hours.

Until July, 1951, the smaller consulting room next door to the waiting room was used by Dr Gilbert Aumont, an experienced radiologist. He spent four months annually carrying out X-ray examinations on behalf of the medical bureau. For this service he received a nominal payment. The writer [F.L.] would like to congratulate and thank him publicly for his services.

It is due to Dr Aumont that facilities have existed over the past three years which have made it possible to undertake 1,500 screenings and an equal number of X-ray photographs.[10]

This number of investigations may seem excessive in view of the few recognised cures. One of the purposes of the Bureau of Scientific Studies is, however, to examine systematically as many patients as possible, so completing as many dossiers as it can for its archives. Over 3,000 cases have accumulated in this way during the three years, 1948, 1949 and 1950. Nor has this been wasted effort. In 1949 there was recorded the case of a child, aged three, afflicted since birth with cerebral diplegia, who was cured three days after her second examination. This alleged cure was to be carefully checked.

The next room is that of the president of the medical bureau. It is larger than the first and more comfortably furnished, and is used for examination of patients. In the intervals between examinations, the doctors present gather there, and during their friendly discussions suggestions are made bearing on the organisation of the medical bureau. It should be understood that the president of the medical bureau is not the whole bureau. His task is to act as liaison officer and administrator and to give continuity to the bureau's activity. The doctors present are themselves responsible for both the intellectual and practical work of the bureau and its continued development is due to their efforts. The writer [F.L.], as president, made no claim to precedence or authority. In his opinion, the president in the medical bureau was just another doctor, a public servant, and if he could be of service to his colleagues his ambition was fulfilled. He prided himself that no one had been inhospitably received there, and that, in its friendly atmosphere, a team spirit and a love of Our Lady had been built up among the members of the International Medical Association of Lourdes, then (1950) totalling nearly 3,000.

Adjoining the president's room is the library. This is a well lighted, well ventilated and roomy apartment. Textbooks of medicine can be found there together with historical documents relating to Lourdes, as can apologetic and fictional matter. Some publishers, realising the value of showing their wares to the large number of medical men who pass through the bureau, have sent it pre-publication copies of their books. In this way the medical bureau is one of the few organisations in the world to receive medical books before they are in circulation.

In addition the library contains the *French Medical Encyclopedia*, which is kept up to date. This has proved so abreast of current developments that the library of the bureau has become a source of reference for the medical men of the district and the rooms are rarely deserted during the summer.

The next room contains a Philips X-ray apparatus. This piece of equipment was installed in 1949 and was then the most modern on the market. It has replaced the former Siemens apparatus, which, while it did yeoman service, could not compare in scope of investigation with the new equipment. The equipment is the gift of the Dutch Catholics, who, stimulated by the director of the Dutch National pilgrimage, have paid the entire cost of manufacture, transport and installation.[11]

Next door to the X-ray department is a room where routine internal examinations (of rectum, cervix uteri, bladder) can be carried out with full aseptic precautions, under direct vision, and where biopsy can be undertaken. This room contains the usual surgical equipment—modern adjustable table, steriliser, etc. There is also apparatus for maintaining and when necessary deflating an artificial pneumothorax. This equipment calls for comment; some doctors have expressed surprise that medical treatment of any kind is undertaken at the Lourdes Medical Bureau. From the point of view of medical ethics, only registered pilgrims are so treated. Like all medical activities carried out here, these services are free of charge; there is never any question of a fee. Furthermore, it is in the general interest to be able to refill a pneumothorax in view of the large number of patients who come to Lourdes with pulmonary tuberculosis and who may require this service.

In the past many doctors from sanatoria have hesitated to allow (and even refused to permit) their patients to come to Lourdes, knowing that the pneumothorax would not be refilled even when such refill fell due during the period of pilgrimage. The timing of a refill is a matter of importance. A delay of three to five days may well permit the pleural surfaces of the lung to become adherent, so contributing to the patient's deterioration. [Dr Leuret, who died in 1954, was himself experienced in sanatorium practice and had carried out this procedure on several thousand patients. We cannot vouch for current practice. Tr.]

In the theatre there is also equipment for the examination of ear, nose and throat cases. There are sometimes specialists in these branches of medicine with a pilgrimage, but in default of a visiting E.N.T. specialist, Dr Minier, of Lourdes (a member of the I.M.A.L.), a specialist himself, sees patients at the bureau or if necessary at his own consulting rooms.

An electrocardiograph was in use in July, 1951. It was presented through the generosity of the French colony in San Francisco. In 1949 one author [F.L.] told Dr Blanquie, a French physician resident in San Francisco, that it was his intention to set up an electrocardiograph in the bureau in view of the large number of heart cases which come to Lourdes in the hope of being cured.

This was simply mentioned in passing, but that generous man, filled with love of Lourdes, obtained on his return to the United States of America the authority of the Archbishop of San Francisco to open a subscription list among the French colony in that town.

In the basement is the darkroom for developing X-ray photographs. This work is done by a radiographic technician. This room is fitted with modern equipment. The basement also contains equipment for ophthalmological examinations, although the bureau has not yet acquired a set of trial lenses.

All this equipment may seem excessive; it is in fact scarcely sufficient to cope with the annual influx of pilgrims and sick.

ROUTINE CLINICAL WORK AT LOURDES

The task of the medical bureau and the Bureau of Scientific Studies is three-fold.

In the two years previous to 1950 the hospitals sheltered 35,000 sick and the medical bureau was visited by more than 3,000 doctors, including many leaders of the profession, both in France and abroad. The sick have included examples of most interesting and unusual diseases.

It would be unfortunate if these two streams of pilgrims were to meet only on the occasion of an alleged miracle. Attention has been drawn to the importance of doctors seeing the greatest possible number of sick during their careers. The opportunity of doing this is, therefore, put before all medical visitors to Lourdes. Sick persons are seen at the Bureau of Scientific Studies every day. The patients are pleased at the interest shown in them and some hope, and expect, to be examined at the bureau.

The following are seen from 9 a.m. to 2 p.m.:

All those who wish to be seen.

As many as possible with incomplete case notes.

As many as possible with an uncertain diagnosis.

As many as possible of medical interest.

In this building doctors contribute to one another's learning. There is no question of organised teaching; there are in the accepted sense no teachers and no students. Exchange of knowledge is mutual, each contributing his share and picking the brains of his colleagues. This gathering of medical men is a sort of international congress, each one benefiting from his neighbour's contribution. In this way it is gradually being appreciated that not only do doctors benefit by the religious environment of Lourdes, but that, other things being equal, the doctor who has been to Lourdes may, from a medical point of view, have the advantage over the doctor who has not. It seems that this is due to Our Blessed Lady, Mother of all true knowledge, who has wished that such meetings should take place, so that the occurrence of unusual phenomena should be supervised and investigated by medical men.

DETECTION OF FRAUDS

Attempted frauds do occur. They are undoubtedly the root cause of the incredulity and suspicion with which many doctors regard the Lourdes phenomena. It is the object of the medical bureau to unmask these frauds. It

is infinitely preferable that this should be done by servants of Our Lady, rather than by her enemies who then
claim that all cures at Lourdes are fraudulent.

Fifty years ago Dr Boissarie was already reacting ener-
getically to frauds who were prepared to fake miraculous
cures for their own ends.

It should be remembered that Our Lady has an ever
present foe in Satan, in whom, unfortunately, many no
longer believe. He does, however, exist; at Lourdes,
probably more than elsewhere, he attempts to neutralise
her ever widening and powerful influence. Even in the
town of Lourdes itself the struggle goes on, this town, of
which it may well be said (despite the affection in which
its populace is rightly held) that it was chosen for a
splendid spiritual destiny but that, being given the choice
between God and Mammon, it chose Mammon. One
cannot serve two masters.

The attempt to undermine Our Lady's purposes is
visible not only in the town but within the domain of the
grotto itself. As Satan cannot prevent Our Lady from
bringing about remarkable cures in proof of God's
goodness and love, he attempts to produce false "cures":
phenomena most impressive at first sight, but unable to
stand up to critical examination, and easily disproved.

Unfortunately such phenomena are expected, hoped
for, and exaggerated by the general public, and are the
object of excessive publicity. There is even a certain
section of the press, always avid for sensational news,
which noisily reports this kind of thing without restraint,
investigation or discernment. In fact such reporting may
be done with cynical pleasure.

When phenomena are branded as fraudulent by those
anxious to examine them scientifically, it is found that
those who have spread the tale of "miracles" abroad have
only succeeded in rendering a disservice to Our Lady and
to Lourdes. These devil's "miracles" are commonly
motivated by wickedness, vanity or a desire for money.

Dr Leuret is the author of the following three examples.

On August 27th, 1947, about fifteen doctors were chatting in the larger room of the old medical bureau when at about 4 p.m. was heard the sound of feet racing up the Gave River sidepath, and excited voices. We dashed to the door and opened it just in time to allow a dishevelled woman to rush in shouting:

"I'm cured! I'm cured!"

She was an odd looking person with jet black hair somewhat disarranged by the bath and her headlong career to the bureau.

Kiss curls framed her face, her eyebrows were plucked, her lips covered with lipstick, her fingernails scarlet. She had made the most of her outward attractions, such as they were.

She was admitted to the main room and there Dr Michael Bressolette, chief physician to the Hôtel-Dieu, Anger, set about taking the usual case history—previous family and personal antecedents, history of the illness and of the cure.

Following this woman came a stout assistant nurse from the baths. She too arrived shouting, "She's cured! She's cured! I saw her cured myself." This seemed good news. Here was an eyewitness. We set about questioning her.

"You really saw her cured, madam? Could you say of what?"

With some embarrassment and hesitation she said:

"Of an anal fistula, doctor."

"An anal fistula! How did you manage to see her cured of that? You must have bathed her upside down. You might have drowned her!"

"Well, sir, that's not quite what I saw."

"Well, why go about shouting you'd seen her cured under your nose? What exactly did you see, then?"

The witness became more confused and bothered. Finally she stammered:

"Well, I saw her go into the bath wearing bloodstained bandages."

"But madam, you must be about forty. Surely by now you're aware that this can happen without an anal fistula being responsible. Come, stop these assertions. In future be more careful in your claims. Only the Medical Bureau of Lourdes has the right to pronounce on a cure. And we are fairly certain that this is not a cure."

Dr Bressolette then read to the assembled doctors the case history he had obtained. The patient interrupted his narrative at intervals to confirm his statements. This done, the lady bade the assembly farewell and made to leave. We called her back.

"You can't leave yet, madam. We've still to examine you."

"Me? Why?"

"To record your cure."

"But doesn't all I've just said do?"

"Not without full examination."

"But I don't want to be examined."

"But then you shouldn't have wasted our time! What did you come here for?"

"I came to have my cure recorded."

"For a cure to be recorded, the patient must be examined. If you don't agree to that, such record as has been taken will simply be torn up."

"So you won't record my cure?"

"No, madam."

This set the lady weeping, and through her tears we heard the words:

"I've been sent on a wild goose chase! If I'd known I'd never have done it!" We pricked up our ears at this. We wondered what sort of trap we were about to fall into. On our insisting on the examination she gave in; five or six of us undertook it.

There was nothing wrong with her; there never had been. When asked to point out where her anal fistula had been she showed us a scar which was certainly no more than the healed incision through which a sebaceous cyst had been removed. It was well up her back, almost between her shoulder blades; certainly there was no question that the anus had been affected. Our displeasure must have been clearly visible in our faces. I said to her firmly:

"Madam, you're lying. What's all this about?"

She looked discomfited, searched the faces of those surrounding her for support, found none and then said:

"Are you the chief here?"

"I am."

"Well, I'll tell you, but not all the rest."

I took her to another room where, little by little, by dint of much patient effort, she unburdened herself.

She had been sent deliberately by an anti-religious organisation in central France in order to obtain a document to the effect that at the Lourdes Medical Bureau miracles were recognised without examination of the person concerned. Our foes have had to descend to such expedients!

Had the care so necessary not been exercised in this case; that care which has been compared by Dr Boissarie to that of an examining magistrate; had we temporised and said we would go into the matter next year, we should have been the object of a press campaign, possibly on a national scale, to which we might have been unable to give the lie and which might have had the most serious consequences.

This, then, was the devil's "pseudo-miracle," the product of wickedness.

Lydia was a sweet young girl of twenty with an open face, a quiet voice, full of innocence. She came rather shyly to the medical bureau.

"Doctor, I think I've been cured. I've been ill in bed for three years, unable to walk. This morning I was able to do so."

That was obvious since she had come on her feet. "What was the matter with you?" "I'm afraid I don't know, doctor." "Where's your medical certificate?" "I haven't any, doctor." "Why is that, young lady?" "I didn't think I'd be cured."

The usual procedure was set in motion; her history being first recorded. She was asked to undress—this she did willingly enough. She was examined.

For a person who hadn't walked for three years her muscles were in excellent tone; in fact one had the impression that they were the muscles of a dancer or athlete accustomed to regular exercise.

"Surely you've been walking for some time; it doesn't seem possible that you should be so fit."

"Honestly, doctor, I've been in bed for three years without walking."

"We simply can't believe that. Take off your shoes."

"But there's nothing wrong with my feet!"

The soles of her feet were those of a person who'd been using them daily for some time. As this incident occurred only eight days after the first, we taxed her firmly:

"You're not telling the truth. You were walking last week. Now what's all this about?"

Her face fell and tears coursed down her cheeks. Through these she told her tale. "Doctor, a young friend of mine from the neighbouring village was miraculously cured last year. When she came home she was kissed by the mayor and blessed by the parish priest and there were flowers and triumphal arches. . . . I wanted it all to happen to me."

Vanity, stupidity; these are aspects of the same thing. The devil is ever ready to try and discredit Our Lady by using our human self-interest and ambition.

The following story illustrates a further aspect of his attack.

On July 18th, 1948, after an absence of twenty-four hours on official business of state, I returned to Lourdes to find everybody radiant and an undercurrent of joy evident. Surprised, I questioned one of the Lourdes nurses.

"Why so pleased? What's been happening?"

"Don't you know? There's been a tremendous miracle. A deaf-mute, son of deaf-mute parents, recovered his speech in the baths. Just your luck not to be there."

"Has he gone?"

"Not yet."

"Then there's no hurry. There never is with miracles. In fact, the more you wait the better. Send him along to see me."

Shortly after, the subject of the alleged cure appeared. He was a boy aged about fifteen with blue eyes and curly hair who gave the impression of slight mental backwardness. His companion was a tall, ungainly fellow aged about thirty, of very dark complexion, with a greasy beret (which he did not take off) on his head. His unusual face was bordered by long side-whiskers; his eyebrows were plucked, his lips painted red, his nails varnished. He was not the sort of person to meet in a dark alley late at night. I could easily visualise him asking for one's money or life.

"Are you related to each other?"

"No, we're not," replied the older man.

"How long have you known him?"

"Three days."

"How do you know he's been deaf and dumb from birth?"

"From his identity card."

A dirty card was produced. On page one I read: "My name is Antonin L., I am a deaf-mute born of deaf-mute parents; please help if you see me in trouble." On page two was a list of everyday requests: "I need food." "I want to go to the lavatory." And so on.

I returned the document. "Well, that seems fair

enough. Still, anyone could lay hands on that sort of document."

I went on with the inquiry. "When did his speech return?"

"The day before yesterday in the baths."

"What did he say?"

"He said: 'I thank Our Lady very much.' " (These words were pronounced with great emphasis by the witness.)

"Splendid," I said, "not one, but two miracles."

"Two miracles?" (He could almost feel the money flowing into his pocket.)

"Of course. Not only has the boy learned to speak, but he's learned grammar as well."

The wretch saw his mistake; in trying to put it right he simply made the situation worse.

"Doctor, try and understand! Just think a moment." (He seemed about to tell me how to examine a patient.) "He's been in a home for deaf-mutes for the past four years."

"That'll do from you," I said sharply. I addressed myself gently to Antonin. "Look, son, you're in Our Lady's country; tell me the truth, how long have you been able to talk?"

"Two years, sir," was the reply.

I saw them both to the door . . . it was 10:30 a.m.

They at once went and bought two thousand post cards and spent the morning writing: "A souvenir of the deaf-mute cured in the baths, July 16th, 1948." This was signed by Antonin and certified as true by his mentor. These they sold in the streets of Lourdes throughout that afternoon at about ten francs each. They sold all of their cards by seven o'clock that evening, making almost 20,000 francs, which the older man took. Antonin received none of this sum.

Not satisfied with this, they then burgled an empty villa near the Pic du Jer. They were caught red-handed

J

and taken to the local jail. "Don't lay hands on us," cried the leader of the party. "We've been miraculously cured." (Note that both of them were now so privileged.)

I made the situation clear to the police officer who telephoned me to find out if these allegations were true.

They spent a short time in prison and then went home. However, sometime after this I received copies of several local newspapers which contained accounts running to two or three columns of the remarkable cure of a deaf-mute in the baths at Lourdes. I wrote to these and to several major French papers putting the true facts before them. Of these only the Catholic *La Croix* of Paris published my letter; the rest did not acknowledge it, with one exception. This letter said: "Dear sir, we have received your letter. If you think we have time to deny all the news we print you are mistaken, for we should never finish." No comment is necessary.

The above events give the staff of the medical bureau the right to maintain and encourage an attitude of suspicion for which they are often blamed. They are even accused of being responsible for the decrease in the number of miracles.

This view needs correcting. The strict attitude of the Lourdes Medical Bureau has been enjoined on us by the Church. The bishops themselves have indicated that this is their wish. Mgr Théas stated quite categorically before the general meeting of the I.M.A.L. in 1949, "Your only task is to tell the truth. You are asked neither to be excessively strict nor too easy going, but to be exact; to furnish the Church with unimpeachable medical reports, so that she may have an opportunity to decide whether or not a miracle has occurred."

In confirmation of this, one may recall the words of a prince of the Church, "One can never be too strict in such matters."

In any case, how can any single medical man thwart Our Lady? If anyone believes there are fewer miracles than there were (which, incidentally, is untrue—since 1939 records exist of about fifteen genuine cures of which several have been officially declared miraculous) the scientific attitude of the medical profession, which serves only to increase the apologetic value of cases, cannot be blamed.

The blame for the decrease in the number of miracles in the modern world rests with ourselves. Faith and holiness are not as strong as they used to be; the crowds of Lourdes have much in common with those that followed Christ in Galilee; they did so more out of curiosity than out of faith or love.

"Pseudo-miracles" stir the crowds just as did those of the magicians of apostolic days, who sought to annul the effects of Christ's and His apostles' miracles. Let us not be misled by the cries of those who publicise their cures (real or alleged) as widely as possible.

Those who have really been miraculously healed fall silent and behave with humility. They have to be sought out to submit to proper medical investigation. Let us recall that Christ Himself, Who scattered miracles about Him, generally told those who benefited from them to remain silent.

THE RECOGNITION OF UNUSUAL CURES

All the above needed saying. In this way it may be claimed with greater firmness that astonishing phenomena do occur, that inexplicable bodily cures have taken place which are outside the normal laws of nature.

Not only has the medical bureau recorded fifteen cures between 1939 and 1949, but the National Medical Council has confirmed seven of these since its inception in 1947.

The following chapters are concerned with some of these as they have been investigated. They have been divided into three groups:

Cures officially recognised as miracles by the diocesan ecclesiastical authorities.

Cures that cannot be explained according to natural science, but which have either not yet been investigated by the ecclesiastical authorities or have not been declared miraculous by them.

Unusual cures of medical interest, not in themselves certainly miraculous, and possibly capable of natural explanation.

Chapter vii

CURES OFFICIALLY RECOGNISED AS MIRACULOUS

In this chapter a full account is given of four officially recognised miracles together with some of the relevant medical and ecclesiastical documents.

FRANCIS PASCAL (1938)

A pilgrimage has gone from Aix-en-Provence to Lourdes almost every year for many years. On August 29th, 1938, the procession was joined at Tarascon by Francis Pascal. Although the boy was only four years old, he was blind and paralysed. This pilgrimage was led by Mgr Roques, Archbishop of Aix, later Cardinal Archbishop of Rennes.

On July 19th, Dr Dardé of Beaucaire certified that he had been attending Francis Pascal, who was suffering from the after effects of meningitis, including paralysis of his lower limbs and complete blindness. His condition had remained stationary for the past four months and gave no signs of yielding to treatment. The child was placed in charge of the pilgrimage nurses. Nothing unusual happened on the journey. The pilgrimage itself passed without incident.

No notice was taken of the fact that the child's health had apparently improved in Lourdes, though this was generally known. Mgr Roque's prudent advice was: "The medical bureau will decide next year whether any cure has occurred or not." The child's ability to see and walk continued to improve at Beaucaire.

On November 9th, 1938, Dr Dardé, who had been supervising the child's progress (as had Dr Jean Roman, the pilgrimage medical officer at the time of the cure), certified that he had examined Francis Pascal on his return from Lourdes and had noted the disappearance of the paralysis and the return of the ability to see. Here is his statement:

"I certify having attended Francis Pascal, aged four, from December 17th, 1937, to June 14th, 1938. I saw this child in consultation with Drs Julian and Barra (Avignon); Dr Dufoix, Jr (Nîmes); and Dr Polge, ophthalmologist (Arles). The child was suffering from an attack of aseptic lymphocytic meningitis.

"When daily medical attention was discontinued (June 14th, 1938) the child's four limbs were paralysed and his visual acuity was nil. He was unable to tell the difference between night and day. Dr Polge's examination in May 1938 led him to make an unfavourable prognosis.

"I was asked to see the child again about August 20th, prior to his joining the Lourdes pilgrimage. His condition remained the same as in June; his limbs were paralysed; his ability to see was nil.

"The child was brought back to see me by his mother on his return from Lourdes. She and the child walked in, hand in hand. I noted the disappearance of the paralysis and the return of vision. Apart from some unsteadiness the child walked normally.

"From that date to this, the child has continued to improve.

"This change in his health took place after an immersion in the baths at Lourdes. It cannot be explained in terms of the ordinary laws of nature."

Dr Julian was asked to examine the patient, and on December 6th, 1938, made out the following certificate:

"I certify having attended Francis Pascal, then aged four, at his home in Beaucaire, in the Rue Camille-Desmoulins.

"He then had an aseptic lymphocytic meningitis; his condition was serious and became worse. His four limbs were paralysed and his visual acuity was nil. The situation appeared desperate.

"Subsequent to a pilgrimage to Lourdes during which the child was put in the baths, a striking improvement in health took place. The child I examined yesterday shows only minor sequelae which may well improve.

"I have personally examined the child and can say that the statement made by my two colleagues is accurate.

"Young Pascal walks and sees normally."

Francis Pascal was on the list of pilgrims for 1939 and it was hoped to bring him before the Lourdes Medical Bureau in August of that year. War was declared just before the pilgrimage was due to leave and it was abandoned. It was not therefore possible to put this plan into operation.

In view of the fact that there was a question of cure and not simply of improved health and that two certificates had been made out by the doctors in charge of the case, Dr Jean Roman (medical officer to the pilgrimage, and familiar with Pascal's history) wrote to the president of the medical bureau, as follows:

Aix, May 17th, 1939.

"I should like to bring to your notice the case of a child taken to Lourdes at the end of August 1938 with the Aix-en-Provence pilgrimage.

"If you consider the case interesting, as I think you will, I should like to demonstrate it at the medical bureau in August 1939.

Yours sincerely,
J. Roman."

The following is Dr Roman's statement:

"Francis Pascal was born on October 2nd, 1934, at Sault, Vaucluse; he lives with his parents in the Rue Camille-Desmoulins, Beaucaire. His father and mother enjoy good health. Nothing significant is present in the child's personal or family history. Birth was normal; there is no history of injuries or acute illness.

"About December 15th, 1937, the child (whose health had hitherto been satisfactory) began to vomit; his eyes became runny and his temperature rose to 38°C. This varied between 38°C. and 39°C. for two or three days and was accompanied by neck rigidity, vomiting and photophobia. Temperature then varied between 38°C. and 40°C. Meningitic symptoms became more obvious. The child was examined by Drs Dardé, Julian and Polge.

"In March 1938 symptoms affecting vision appeared, as did limb paralysis. Lumbar puncture was carried out by Dr Lesbres, of Avignon. Here is his report:

Macroscopically, the fluid is a little cloudy.
Cytological examination: leucocytes, 125 cu. mm.
    Of these 50% are lymphocytes, 50% polynuclear leu-
    cocytes.

Albumen 0·62%. Glucose 0·33%.
W.R.—negative.
Tubercle bacilli not found; no other organisms found.
Culture: negative on solid ascitic medium after six days'
    incubation.

"The child was seen regularly by his attending physicians until June 1938. He then had complete paralysis of his four limbs and was totally blind; he could neither distinguish night from day nor appreciate light.

"Dr Polge (Ophthalmologist) made the following statement in May 1938: 'This child was brought to me because he was both paralysed and unable to see. The pupils reacted to light only slightly; neither a light nor anything else moved back and forth in front of the eyes was ever followed. Examination of the fundus showed congested veins and some degree of optic pallor. These findings led me to make an extremely guarded prognosis in view of the time which had elapsed since the original infection.'

"I [Dr Roman] saw the child again in June 1938 on the occasion of a pilgrimage to Frigolet (Our Lady of Good Healing). He was blind and unable to use his limbs; his lower limbs were flaccid; his upper limbs moved in an unco-ordinated way.

"I saw him again on the 1938 Lourdes pilgrimage (Aix-en-Provence diocese). I noted he was still in the same condition, i.e. blind and with his lower limbs paralysed. Dr Dardé had supplied the following certificate. 'I, the undersigned, Dr Dardé, certify that I have been attending Francis Pascal, aged four, suffering from the sequelae of meningitis, namely paralysis of the lower limbs and total blindness. These lesions appear to be in a stationary condition and seem uninfluenced by treatment.'

"I was medical officer in charge of the pilgrimage train and can confirm that this certificate was accurate. The child travelled as a stretcher case and could neither detect light nor objects presented to him.

"At Lourdes he was put in the baths; his mother was present and it appears that his reaction was severe, for she thought he had had a fit. He was bathed again next day without incident. Both the mother and a lady helper who accompanied the child state that on their way across the esplanade after this bath the child apparently began to see and pointed out a tricycle to his mother. Again, on the train journey home he seemed to be able to see.

"Dr Dardé, who saw the child before he left for Lourdes, stated on his return: 'Mme Pascal brought the child back to see me on his return from Lourdes; the child was able to walk. I noted that the paralysis had disappeared and vision had returned. The child walked normally apart from a little unsteadiness.' In November, Dr Dardé added that 'this improvement has been maintained and has increased.'

"These observations are borne out by those of Dr Julian, of Tarascon, who had seen him in March 1938. He stated: 'This child had had an aseptic lymphocytic meningitis. His condition was serious and became worse. His four limbs were paralysed and his visual acuity was nil. The situation was desperate. After a pilgrimage to Lourdes, during which the child was bathed, a considerable improvement occurred. The child I saw yesterday showed only minor sequelae which may well improve. I saw the child in December 1938, when he was walking normally and could see things around him.' "

Owing to the war, during which all pilgrimages stopped, Dr Roman was unable to read the report until October 2nd, 1946. Eleven doctors were present in Lourdes, including two lecturers in medical faculties and an assistant professor at Val-de-Grâce.

Subsequent to this report Dr Vallet made the following statement:

"This year (1946) the Aix diocesan pilgrimage, 900 persons under the leadership of its archbishop, Mgr Charles de Provenchères, came to Lourdes. Owing to personal circumstances Francis Pascal himself was unable to attend. Dr Roman, however, in reading his report, showed several photographs, including one taken recently.

"Francis Pascal, now in his twelfth year, seems a healthy little boy, apparently normal in height and with well-developed muscles. He rides a bicycle and goes to ordinary school. This is what Dr Roman, who knows him well, says: 'It seems from inspection of the documents put before us that the child clearly suffered from an organic infectious disorder of the meninges. The ophthalmic lesions and the response of the C.S.F. support a diagnosis of organic disease. The infection fits into that group of virus disorders of the central nervous system of unknown origin. In reply to the usual questions the following answers can be given:

"There can be no doubt concerning the reality of the illness. It was an infection involving the meninges, nervous system and optic nerve, associated with papilloedema, flaccid paralysis of the lower limbs and inco-ordination of the upper limbs. Symptoms of cerebellar disorder were also present.

"Symptoms cleared up suddenly when the progress of the disease gave no reason to hope for improvement. On the second day of bathing the child was able to see a tricycle and by the time he reached home he was able to walk.

"Recovery is undoubted as evidenced by return of vision, ability to walk and ability to undertake physical activity.

"There is no need to delay decision that a cure has taken place since it has now lasted for eight years.

"No medical explanation appears possible of the sudden disappearance of the illness and its symptoms."

This document is signed by eleven doctors in addition to Dr Vallet, the president of the bureau, and is dated October 2nd, 1946.

Francis Pascal came to Lourdes with the diocesan pilgrimage from Nîmes in 1947 and 1948, when he was seen and examined at the medical bureau by fifteen doctors, who confirmed the above findings Dr Leuret, who had succeeded Dr Vallet as president of the bureau, saw the patient on each of these occasions. He again recorded the history of the illness, noting that it was an infective meningitic syndrome associated with paralysis of all four limbs and serious visual disturbances. He recorded the improvement following the bathing, and the fact that the child regained his sight and ability to move (Cf. Dr Dardé's statement after the pilgrimage). Dr Leuret concluded as follows: "This cure has been sent before the canonical commission of the patient's diocese for its decision. It cannot be explained in ordinary terms, particularly in view of the nature of the illness itself, the permanence of the lesions recorded, the sudden return of sight and power of locomotion."

On March 27th, 1947, the Archbishop of Aix instructed Mgr Monnier, his vicar general, to investigate the cure of Francis Pascal. The canonical commission was made up as follows:

President: Mgr Hippolyte Monnier.
Promoter of the faith: Canon Louis Coste, rector of the senior seminary.
Secretary: Fr Joseph Mouly, spiritual director of the senior seminary.
Consultors: Fr Franck; Canon Marcel Andrieux, rector of the junior seminary.

Each member of this body examined the file referring to Francis Pascal, which had been passed to them by the medical bureau. The documents concerned were fully discussed at several sittings. The "degree of pallor" of the optic discs mentioned by Dr Polge led the commission to request a further investigation into this matter. The child was therefore examined by Dr Bayle, ophthalmologist to the Arles hospitals and successor to Dr Polge. Having gone into the case and taken note of the certificates issued by the attending physicians, he stated:

"I have today (April 26th, 1948) seen Francis Pascal, aged thirteen and a half, for the first time. He looks a strong, healthy lad showing no evidence of physical or mental abnormality. I have been asked to examine him from an ophthalmological point of view.

"There is present a secondary optic atrophy; there has been recovery of visual acuity to 1 and 0·2. This permits normal vision, a state of affairs which has been present apparently for ten years, since his remarkably rapid cure."

According to Dr Bayle, therefore, there had been a restoration of visual acuity.

The commission then turned its attention to the question of whether this was a miraculous cure or not.

On December 10th, 1949, the commission heard Fr Franck's statement. This was agreed to at the final meeting on December 18th. Fr Mouly, the secretary, summarised the work done as follows:

"Having taken these facts into consideration and having studied the case notes afresh (after they had been studied by each of the commission's members individually) the commission concluded unanimously that the cure of Francis Pascal, in the present state of scientific knowledge, cannot be explained in natural terms; and that it is the result of a specific intervention of God. Fr Franck was directed on December 10th to draw up a final draft of the commission's report. This was read and approved by the commission on December 18th, 1948. The commission submitted its findings to the archbishop, inviting him to declare the cure of Francis Pascal miraculous." [This statement was signed by the members of the commission.]

Fr Franck's report was divided into three parts: the facts of the illness; a critical, historical and medical assessment; and the conclusion, which follows:

"Critical examination (of the facts) from the theological standpoint. In view of the above facts [this refers to Parts I and II of the report], we can say that, at Lourdes, Francis Pascal was the beneficiary of a maternal intervention on the part of Our Blessed Lady and that his return to a permanent state of normal health must be attributed to this intervention.

"But is this a true miracle in the strict theological meaning of the term? In other words, is all possible explanation by natural causes ruled out so as to point directly, inexorably and exclusively to the action of the First Cause, to God Himself acting through the all-powerful intercession of Mary Immaculate?

"Basing our conclusions on those of Dr Dardé and many other doctors concerned in the proceedings of the Lourdes Medical Bureau, we consider that this is a true miracle and that the answer (to the first question above) is in the affirmative.

"We may add that these conclusions are in accord with the principles laid down by Benedict XIV concerning such matters; namely that there did exist an illness, serious in nature, of organic origin, without hope of cure, unresponsive to treatment, considered desperate, in which no remedy had been used for months.

"The cure was sudden, taking place after the second immersion in the bath at Lourdes. This complete cure has been maintained for the past ten years. As no treatment had preceded this event, as it was organic in nature and as it had occurred in a child aged four, it cannot be attributed to any cause in the normal order of things.

"May it, therefore, please your Excellency to declare as miraculous the cure of Francis Pascal, which took place at Lourdes on August 31st, 1938, due to the intercession of Mary Immaculate, ever powerful before her Blessed Son.

H. Monnier, vicar general; Louis Coste; J. Mouly; M. Andrieux; G. Franck."

This document, together with the complete file, was submitted to the archbishop by the vicar general, Mgr Monnier, on December 20th, 1948.

The archbishop made his decision known publicly (after much prayer and thought) on May 31st, 1949.[1]

"Charles de Provenchères, by the Grace of God and favour of the Apostolic See, Archbishop of Aix, Arles and Embrun, to the clergy and faithful of our diocese:

"Greetings and blessing in the name of Our Lord Jesus Christ.

"In August 1938 a child less than four years old was taken to Lourdes with the archdiocesan pilgrimage of Aix. His name was Francis Pascal, born on October 2nd, 1934; he was blind and his limbs were paralysed.

"The child had been supplied by his attending physician with a certificate to the effect that he was suffering from the 'sequelae of meningitis, including paralysis of the lower limbs and complete blindness,' and that these appeared unaffected by any form of treatment. Dr Roman, medical officer to the pilgrimage, confirmed the accuracy of this statement.

"On August 31st, 1938, after a second immersion in the baths, the child's sight and use of his limbs returned. On his return from Lourdes he was seen by Dr Dardé who recorded the cure and stated that 'such a phenomenon cannot be explained in medical terms.'

"Time has confirmed the cure. As no pilgrimage to Lourdes took place during the war, the relevant medical documents were not submitted to the Lourdes Medical Bureau until 1946. At that session the eleven doctors present stated: 'No medical explanation can be given of the sudden disappearance of the child's symptoms and paralysis.'

"The child was seen at Lourdes in July, 1947, by fifteen doctors, including four from teaching hospitals, who confirmed the previous findings.

"At our request the case was again gone into at the Lourdes Medical Bureau on September 1st, 1948. We ourselves were there during the discussion by the twenty medical men present and inquired if they considered that they had before them the necessary medical documents to reach a decision concerning the case.

"All answered in the affirmative; they assured us that, after careful examination of the relevant documents, no doubt could exist from the medical point of view. They signed the proceedings of the meeting. Here is its conclusion: 'The doctors here present confirm the previous findings concerning Francis Pascal's cure. In 1938 he was blind and paralysed; today he can see and walk. This change dates from his visit to Lourdes (August 31st, 1938). We declare that this cure cannot be explained in natural terms, that it took place unrelated to the use of drugs and that it has lasted ten years. In a word, it does not fit in with the laws of nature.'

"We had meanwhile set up a canonical commission to investigate the truth of the above facts and to come to such conclusions as could be drawn from the findings of Lourdes Medical Bureau. This body was made up of our vicar general, Mgr Monnier; Rev. Canons Coste and Andrieux, heads of our senior and junior seminaries respectively; Fr Mouly, lecturer at the senior seminary and Fr Franck, former lecturer in the French seminary in Rome.

"The commission issued its findings in December 1948. This includes a very careful investigation of the facts, the medical certificates and the proceedings of the Lourdes Medical Bureau. It concludes as follows: 'There is a superabundance of witnesses and proofs to the effect that a serious illness was present in this case and that the patient was undoubtedly cured in a way which cannot be naturally explained.' [Here follows Fr Franck's report from the words "But is this a true miracle . . ." see p. 141.]

"In view of the above; in view of the medical certificates relating to the case, particularly those of Dr Dardé, dated July 19th, 1938, November 9th, 1938, and June 5th, 1939, and that of Dr Julian, dated December 6th, 1938;

"In view of the proceedings of the Lourdes Medical Bureau, dated October 2nd, 1946, and September 1st, 1948;

"In view of the findings of the canonical commission set up by us, dated December 10th and 18th, 1948;

"Having invoked the name of God:

"In virtue of the authority delegated to us by the Council of Trent and in all things submitting our decision to the authority of the Sovereign Pontiff;

"We decide and declare that Francis Pascal was miraculously cured at Lourdes on August 31st, 1938, and this phenomenon must be ascribed to the special intervention of the Blessed and Immaculate Virgin Mary, Mother of God.

"Given at Aix, this 31st day of May, 1949, on the feast of Our Blessed Lady, Mediatrix of all Graces.

✠ Charles, Archbishop of Aix, Arles and Embrun.
By order of his Excellency.

E. Martin, chancellor.

"This decree will be read in all churches and chapels of the diocese on a Sunday or other day set aside in honour of the Blessed Virgin. The 'Magnificat' will be sung to thank Our Mother in heaven for a miracle which has manifested her power and maternal love."

GABRIELLE CLAUZEL (1943)

On February 11th, 1948, Mgr Lacaste, Bishop of Oran, appointed a committee to investigate the healing of Gabrielle Clauzel, which occurred on August 15th, 1943, in the parish church of Palissy, Oran. On March 18th, 1948, the five members of the committee unanimously confirmed the miraculous character of the cure. Herewith is the report of Dr Maurin, honorary surgeon of the city hospital of Oran, and of Dr Vallet, president at that time of the Medical Bureau of Lourdes:

"Mlle Clauzel, Rue d'Alsace-Lorraine, Oran, was admitted to hospital in 1937 for a rectovaginal fistula which had developed following a hemorrhoidal abscess. She suffered a relapse and required further surgical treatment.

"While in hospital she had an acute attack of rheumatism of the joints. Her left wrist in particular was affected; it was painful and very swollen. Other joints were affected, particularly those of her cervical vertebrae.

"These inflammatory lesions settled down and her condition improved after a spell at Aix-les-Bains. She remained in this state for about a year, throughout which she walked with a stoop. She then had to go back to bed. There were no inflammatory phenomena as on the first occasion, but she complained of lumbar and cervical pains. X-rays taken at this date showed osteophytes ('parrot beaks') to be present, deformities of the vertebral bodies typical of osteoarthritic (rheumatic) spondylitis.

"At this period the patient developed attacks, sometimes violent, of generalised myoclonic spasms, but without loss of consciousness, nor with any associated change in the colour of her face. These attacks often started for no apparent reason but might be set off by an injection or sudden movement. They were sometimes frequent but their intensity was variable, though they were occasionally so violent and lasted sufficiently long to need an inhalation of Kelene to arrest them.

"All the usual sedatives were ineffective in these circumstances. At intervals the patient was given intravenous injections of salicylate of iodaseptine (five ml. every second day). She had no bouts of temperature in these attacks, though her temperature had risen and fallen rapidly during the first attack. She was unable to sit and quite unable to get up. Any attempt to get her to do so resulted in myoclonic attacks.

"A consultant (Dr Porot) from the Faculty of medicine of Algiers was asked to see the patient. He took note of her state without arriving at a firm diagnosis or the cause of her symptoms.

"At this examination he was able to persuade the patient to stand upright out of bed for a few minutes, with support. The nervous reflexes gave no positive diagnostic help.

"Antirheumatic measures were continued.

"A few days after Dr Porot's examination the patient was persuaded to get up and even sit in an armchair. The myoclonic seizures seemed to have disappeared completely, but she was unable to walk. This improvement lasted only a short while, and the patient returned to bed complaining of pain in the region of the lumbar and cervical spine and radiating to the right iliac fossa. This symptom had been noted some years previously and had resulted in her appendix being removed.

"These painful crises were ill-defined and bore no resemblance to renal or biliary colic. No abnormality was ever detected in the urine. The abdomen was a little distended but no sign enabling a firm diagnosis to be made could be elicited. The crises occurred at frequent intervals and produced a

K

crouching attitude in the patient. By now the myoclonic crises had completely disappeared. This state of affairs lasted several months and the patient could no longer be got out of bed even in her better moments.

"At about this time she developed symptoms and signs of gastric disturbance consisting of hyperchlorhydria,[2] vomiting (the latter being sometimes bilious in character) and marked anorexia which reduced her food intake to small proportions. X-rays of stomach and gall bladder taken at about this period were negative. These symptoms stopped quite suddenly and were followed by attacks of indefinite precordial pain radiating toward the shoulder but not accompanied by angor animi, though dyspnoea was occasionally present. This group of symptoms disappeared and bladder pains developed; the patient suffered from retention of urine needing regular catheterisation and an indwelling catheter which was necessary for several months. At the end of this period the catheter was removed and normal micturition returned. The kidneys were at no time tender or enlarged; urinary examination was always negative. This was toward the end of 1943.

"The patient's condition did not improve; she was still confined to bed, complaining of severe pains in the right iliac fossa and the renal area; these painful crises were now worse and needed many pain-relieving injections. The pain now spread round the right hypochondrium but never became a true girdle pain. Palpation of the biliary area gave rise to pain. Her digestive symptoms became worse, anorexia being nearly complete, and very little food was taken. She became extremely thin, her breath smelled strongly of acetone and her pulse was rapid and feeble.

"She was given an infusion of glucose serum and a small amount of insulin to combat the acidosis.

"In this precarious condition she was taken home by her family; Dr Pamart of Bel-Abbès was of the opinion that she would live only a short time.

"On the morning of the 15th of August, 1943, the feast of the Assumption, the patient was taken to attend mass. After this was over she announced that she wished to get up, which she did, to the surprise of her relatives; she walked alone in the church and arrived home without being exhausted—her home being a few hundred yards from the church. She ate a meal with zest; has since then experienced no discomfort; and has eaten steadily and gained several kilogrammes in weight.

"Before coming to any conclusion this long statement must be carefully analysed.

"It can be claimed with confidence that the patient suffered from attacks of acute rheumatism as evidenced by numerous periarticular swellings of an inflammatory nature. This diagnosis is supported by the X-ray findings which indicated spondylitis associated with many 'parrot beak' osteophytes.[3] The crises from which the patient suffered were very variable in their symptomatology. They consisted of severe myoclonic attacks involving most of the muscles of the body. These were followed by attacks of pain in the right iliac fossa, which recurred throughout the illness and became particularly severe toward its end.

"Then came the praecordial attacks of pain, lasting several months, which suddenly disappeared, never to return. These were followed by retention of urine requiring an indwelling catheter for several months. This was succeeded by the alimentary symptoms; the pain in the right hypochondrium causing the patient to lie doubled up; by acidosis—suggestive of defective liver function—and by vomiting, all of which made the patient's condition most alarming.

"These observations cannot fail at first sight to suggest a functional psychological disorder; the myoclonic attacks, the appearance and disappearance of pain; the variable nature of the latter; the absence of positive findings in the examination of the nervous system; the absence of Babinski's sign.

"In addition the patient's state could be altered—though only temporarily—by a strong emotional stimulus, e.g. the examination by Dr Porot was followed by lively and imperious words on the part of the patient. While such stimuli could bring about a marked change in her attitude, this was always fleeting.[4]

"Furthermore, two operations in which some osteophytes were removed were undertaken in the hope of helping the patient psychologically, as she thought they were responsible for her illness and their removal might cure her. These surgical interventions were without effect.

"However, it seems not unlikely that the clinical picture corresponds with a diagnosis of compression of the spinal roots at different levels. The whole vertebral column showed abnormalities of a pathological nature.[5] Both the visceral and other manifestations of pain fit in with this conclusion.

"Finally it is clear that Mlle Clauzel, who was one day so ill as to make it seem probable she would soon be dead, could on the next day get off her stretcher unassisted, walk about her own home without any suffering and eat at table with her family. These findings make it reasonable to suppose that she cannot have been cured so completely and swiftly except by some supernatural agent." (See Appendix 2 for the medical translator's remarks about this point.)

The report of the Lourdes Medical Bureau, dated August 19th, 1945, follows:

"Mlle Chauzel was seen on the above date by the doctors present in the bureau. Dr Maurin's report was read. According to him the case was one of compression of the spinal nerve roots at various levels associated with a diffuse rheumatic spondylitis. The compression appears to have given rise to the pains, at first intermittently and then continuously, the pains becoming more severe in nature with the passage of time. They occurred almost throughout the whole body involving muscles, cervical region, thoracic and lumbar vertebral regions, precordial, vesical and renal areas and gastric and hepatic areas. These latter pains apparently occurred subsequent to some defect of function in the alimentary tract which gradually became worse as judged by the anorexia, intolerance to all forms of food and defective liver function. This alimentary failure became so serious as to lead to the death of the patient being expected at any moment, till the cure itself.

"Mlle Clauzel was examined in order to confirm that she had been operated upon for removal of several 'parrot beaks.' Three scars were found in the midline of the lower cervical, midthoracic and upper lumbar vertebral regions.

"The spinal column as a whole was free of tenderness to percussion; flexion, extension and lateral movements could be fully performed."

ROSE MARTIN (1947)

A statement signed by Dr Strobino of Nice, on behalf of the Bureau of Scientific Studies, is presented herewith:[6]

"Mme Rose Martin, aged forty-five, had suffered since November 1945 from clinical features suggestive of cervical carcinoma. These included metrorrhagia, menorrhagia and, on vaginal examination, an indurated lesion which bled freely on being handled.

"On February 19th, 1946, she was operated on (Dr Fay's wards) in the Pasteur Hospital, Nice, when an extensive hysterectomy was done. Pathological examination of the tissues removed showed it to be an epithelioma of the cervix uteri.

"She developed a hernia of the abdominal wall and on October 4th she was again operated on to deal with this and a fistulous track which had also formed.

"Fourteen months later (April 24th, 1947) she was seen again complaining of alimentary symptoms. She was unable to pass a motion without the use of enemata; the results of this procedure were made up of fœtid matter. She also complained of attacks of pain in the region of the rectum which radiated down her legs. Rectal examination revealed the presence of a swelling about the size of a small orange, at about the upper border of the rectum, on the anterior wall. The swelling could also be detected through the abdominal wall.

"The patient's general health was now very poor. She was extremely cachectic and had been bedridden for several months. She passed a great deal of foul-smelling matter *per vaginum.*

"In view of the clinical features of the case and of the patient's previous history, the surgeon in charge diagnosed spread of the cancer to the rectum and considered biopsy unnecessary. Her serious condition ruled out any radical therapy; the pain in the rectal area necessitated four daily injections of 8 cg. of morphine.

"On June 30th, 1947, the patient was taken to Lourdes in

an advanced state of disease, very cachectic and almost coma-
tose. On the journey she needed repeated injections of
camphor.

"After the third bath (July 3rd, 1947) she wanted to be
bathed without assistance, despite the fact that she had been
unable to stand for several months. That same evening she
went to the lavatory herself and passed a normal motion
without the need for an enema. From that time she has passed
no purulent matter at all, nor has she suffered any pain. Her
appetite has since been exceptionally good.

"Dr Fay saw her again in Nice. He recorded that both the
tumour and signs of disordered function had disappeared.

"Since then all her pains have vanished, her bowels are open
daily, she no longer suffers from vaginal loss, her appetite is
supranormal.

"She remained addicted to the injections of morphine.
However, her requirements became gradually less, and the
injections stopped in January, 1948.

"Her doctors see her regularly each year. She put on
37 lbs. in ten months and leads an active life as a housewife.

"On March 10th, 1948, a barium enema indicated that her
rectum was intact; her vagina was quite soft and normal.

"She was seen again at Lourdes on July 6th, 1948, by many
doctors at the medical bureau. She was in excellent health and
had put on fifty-five pounds in a year. Dr Leuret passed a
rectoscope and found her rectum quite normal.

"She was seen again on February 4th, 1949, by Dr Fay,
who found her in first-class health."

[The medical translator saw Mme Martin in the summer
of 1949. She was a placid, rather unresponsive, slightly
obese lady. On examination her abdomen revealed a long
median scar which was quite healthy. Deep palpation of
her abdomen—it was almost possible to run one's hands
round her pelvis—produced no tenderness and revealed
no tumour. She had no complaints. She informed her
examiner that she had not at the time of her cure been a
practising Catholic. According to a recent newspaper
report she still does not attend Mass.]

JEANNE FRETEL (1948)

The report of the Rennes Canonical Commission to the Cardinal Archbishop of Rennes (November 4th, 1950) follows:

"On September 10th, 1950, you set up a canonical commission, on which the undersigned have served, to investigate the cure of Mlle Jeanne Fretel (auxiliary nurse), of 90 Boulevard de Verdun, who was cured in the course of the Rosary pilgrimage to Lourdes on October 8th, 1948. She remained well throughout 1949 and the National Medical Commission recognised her cure on March 12th, 1950.

"Your commission has the honour to submit its findings, conclusions and recommendations.

"Two points emerge from this inquiry:

"1. The evidence of the person concerned and of the medical witnesses make it clear that a cure has occurred.

"2. The unusual character of the cure puts it beyond the laws of nature.

"Mlle Jeanne Fretel (born May 27th, 1914, at Sougeal), has a long history of poor health. She contracted measles, scarlet fever and diphtheria in childhood.

"In January, 1938, she was operated on (Hôtel-Dieu, Rennes) for appendicitis.[7]

"She was in hospital for a month; she came back the following August, because abdominal pains had recurred. These were accompanied by a gradual, firm and doughy distention of the abdomen. Ultraviolet light treatment resulted in some improvement and she went to live with relatives for some months. But in January, 1939, the patient, now quite bedridden, was admitted for the third time to the Hôtel-Dieu where Dr Maruelle removed an adherent tuberculous ovarian cyst. The post-operative course was satisfactory and the wound healed quickly.

"In September, however, the abdominal pains returned more acutely.

"On March 18th, 1940, she was again admitted to the Hôtel-Dieu. The pain was unsuccessfully treated with ice bags. A diagnosis of tuberculous peritonitis was made by the attending surgeon, who performed a laparotomy in May, 1941. This resulted in the formation of a stercoral fistula without any general improvement in the patient's condition. Four attempts at closure of the fistula failed (12-41, 9-42, 7-43, 9-43).

"In November, 1944, the fistula was successfully closed. Despite this, the abdomen remained tense and swollen.

"On January 31st, 1946, the patient was admitted to a sanatorium. (Pessac, Gironde, 31/1/46—24/4/46). She then went to the sanatorium of La Benne-Océan (Landes) where she remained from April to December, 1946. She continued to deteriorate.

"At La Benne-Océan she underwent two operations: on July 5th, 1946, for bilateral hallux valgus; on July 16th for suppurative osteitis of the upper jaw. She was left with only three upper and six lower teeth.

"All these operations produced great weariness in the patient, and she became very thin. As a result of her poor general health she returned on December 3rd, 1946, to the hospice at Pontchaillon—'to die'—her own words. She was given Extreme Unction (she had received it once before, in 1942). She had by now been in bed for a year and could not get up. Her temperature varied from 39·5°C. (a.m.) to 36·5°C. (p.m.). A tender, doughy mass could be palpated through her distended abdominal wall. She was getting 600 mg. of morphine daily by injection.

"In April, 1948, Dr Pellé, as a last resort, gave the patient a forty-five-day course of streptomycin, which relieved the pain. But she continued to bring up black vomit. The temperature fell with this treatment but rose once more to 40°C., then fell to 36°C. and one evening to 35·9°C. According to the case notes, the patient became steadily less strong from August to October, 1948, and was able to consume only minimal amounts of food.

"Signs of meningeal involvement appeared and her abdomen remained ballooned and very tender.

"The stools contained abundant pus, while the material vomited contained altered (black) blood. Cardiovascular collapse threatened the patient's life and all hope of recovery had been abandoned.

"On September 20th, 1948 (the third time in five years),

the last sacraments were administered; 200 mg. of morphine three to four times a day were still needed.

"The patient left for Lourdes on October 4th, 1948, with a full-blown tuberculous peritonitis and signs of meningeal involvement. She was very cachectic. She went with the Rosary pilgrimage, from Rennes, in a state of complete exhaustion.

"She was unaware that she was on the way to Lourdes. She vomited continuously. Dr Hylli (Landivisiau), who looked after her during the journey, gave her two injections of morphine.

"The patient arrived at Lourdes on Tuesday, October 5th, attended Mass at the grotto and was bathed on the 6th and 7th; no change in her condition was noted.[8]

"On Friday, October 8th, she was taken in a moribund condition to St Bernadette's altar where Mass was being said for the sick. The celebrant hesitated to give her Holy Communion on account of the vomiting and weakness. However, on the stretcher-bearer's insistence, he gave her a small piece of the Host.

"At that moment, she informs us, she felt well and realised she was at Lourdes. 'I was asked how I felt; I said I felt fine. My stomach was still tense and swollen, but I no longer suffered any pain. I was given a cup of coffee which I took eagerly, and kept down. After Mass I was taken to the grotto on my stretcher. On reaching it I felt myself apparently helped into a sitting position. I glanced round to see who had helped me but there was no one there. I now felt as if someone was guiding my hands to my stomach. I wondered what was happening and whether I was cured or dreaming. I found my stomach normal and suddenly felt very hungry.'[9]

"On her return to the hospital by stretcher she told the ward chaplain (Rev. Fr Blancherie, O.P., of Rennes) that she felt very well and that her stomach was no longer full. He measured the slack of her belt and agreed that a change had taken place. She asked for food.

"Dr Guegan (Saint-Mé-en-le-Grand) examined her and allowed her to be fed. She ate well, the meal consisting of veal, mashed potatoes and three slices of bread. She had not had as good a meal for ten years.

" 'I was still hungry after this meal and asked for more food; when I'd finished this I wanted still more. I was given a dish of rice; it was then considered I'd had enough. All this food stayed down.'

"Next afternoon the patient rose, dressed and went to the baths. 'I hadn't walked for three years, and I walked as well then as I do now. At the baths I had a bath myself without feeling tired.'

"She ate well that evening nor did she wake during the night except to ask for food at 11 p.m. After her meal she fell asleep again.

"Next day (Saturday, October 9th) she was taken to the medical bureau on a stretcher. There she was examined by five doctors. One of these, Dr Guyon of Nantes, unaware that she had walked about on the previous night, said 'If you're better as you claim, let's see if you can get up and walk.'

" 'They wanted to help me, but I refused and got up and walked. On noticing how thin I was (my legs looked like match-sticks), Dr Guyon came toward me as if he thought I'd fall, but I didn't. The doctor walked quickly away from me toward the weighing machine; despite his quick walk I kept up with him and was found to weigh 102 pounds. I was told to come back next year.'

"The return journey did not tire her. 'I was up a long time in the train, seeing the sick. Someone wanted to give me morphine with the object of reducing my need for it gradually, but I didn't need it and could rest at will. I returned to work on reaching home. Since my cure at Lourdes, I've always been as well as I am now. I've needed no medicines since.'

"Mlle Fretel's statements are confirmed by doctors who examined her at Lourdes and, on her return, at Rennes.

"She was examined the day after her cure at the medical bureau at Lourdes. The inquiry confirmed the details given above. The circumference of the abdomen (39 inches before the cure) was (at that examination) 30 inches. She was able to walk for the first time since October 17th, 1945. Palpation revealed a soft, supple, painless abdomen. No abnormality was detected except atrophy of the lower limbs.

"Dr Pellé states: 'We saw Mlle Jeanne Fretel on the day of her return from Lourdes to Rennes. We examined her and recorded the complete disappearance of all pathological signs; we have seen her regularly and noted the steady improvement in her general health. On October 9th, 1948, she weighed 102 pounds; she now weighed 124 pounds. This young woman put on almost three pounds daily for the first eight days after her cure. Her temperature is normal, 38·8°C. (a.m.), 37·2°C.— 37·3°C. (p.m.). She eats and sleeps well. Jeanne Fretel was able to take up active work the day after her cure. She is working to this day without anything abnormal happening to her.

"She has since had no pain; normal life and full health have returned. She is up from 5.30 a.m. to 11 p.m. daily. She has the job with the heaviest duties in the house.

"On October 5th, 1949, the patient was examined by Drs Debroise of Rennes, Taillefer of Béziers, Guyon of Nantes, Ricusset of Montpellier and Valdignié of Toulouse.

"The circumference of the abdomen was then twenty-eight inches and the patient weighed over 128 pounds. They noted that the illness had been suddenly halted at a time where no improvement seemed likely. All symptoms of disease had disappeared. A cure had taken place which apparently could not be attributed to medicines. Streptomycin, which had been used for six weeks without effect, had been stopped four months before cure. No medical explanation could account for this cure: it was considered outside the laws of nature.

"It is hardly surprising that after it had examined the relevant documents the National Medical Commission should make the following statement (session held March 12th, 1950): 'The remarkable history of this illness, the size of the medical file (thirty temperature charts, including eighteen before and twelve after cure), the quality of the medical practitioners who have seen the patient, the very detailed observations which are recorded daily from April to October, 1948, the rise in weight (thirty-one pounds in a year), all claim close attention, and enable us to conclude that an inexplicable cure has taken place.'

"The patient's own account of events, the witness of the attending doctors, and of the specialists concerned, make Mlle Fretel's case outstanding (in the opinion of the medical men) and puts it outside the limits of natural laws. The three main reasons for this view are:

"1. No treatment specifically relevant to the disease had been given for several months before the cure.

"2. The instantaneous nature of the cure.

"3. The complete absence of convalescence.

"The doctors' own statement indicates that the illness ended suddenly; all symptoms vanished, while no streptomycin had been given for the previous four months.

"The dying patient, unaware of her journey to Lourdes, became lucid there and felt cured shortly after receiving a portion of the Blessed Sacrament at St Bernadette's altar. Her suffering had ended and she was able to keep down a cup of coffee. Shortly after her arrival at the grotto she noted that her abdomen had returned to normal. She ate a large meal at lunchtime. In the afternoon she walked to the baths, despite the fact that she had not walked for several years and despite the extreme thinness of her legs. She remained up for a long time on the return journey without weariness and visited the sick. Despite the fact that on her return to Rennes she undertook heavy work, she put on almost twenty-four pounds in the first eight days after cure. There was no intervening period between her illness, which had apparently reached its premortal stage, and complete recovery of health. She has been so fit since that time that she has hardly needed even an aspirin.

"Mlle Fretel's story, with all its accompaniment, is one of those extraordinary facts which cannot be accounted for by natural science and in the face of which one can only repeat, 'Here God's hand has rested.'

"Given Mlle Jeanne Fretel's cure, which she has sincerely described under oath;

"Given Dr Pellé's statements and conclusions which are embodied in a long account of the various stages of the disease covering the period January, 1938, to October 9th, 1948 (the date of Mlle Fretel's cure), and given the excellent health she has enjoyed since then;

"Given the statements and conclusions of the commission of medical experts and of the medical bureau reached at the latter's two examinations (October 9th, 1948, and October 5th, 1949), whose findings have been confirmed by the Paris Medical Commission at its meeting on March 12th, 1950;

"Given the distinguishing features of this cure, namely, the sudden and complete disappearance of a normally deadly illness (the patient's demise seemed imminent), without the use of any curative agent and with no period of convalescence (facts vouched for by doctors of unimpeachable authority), all of which indicate with certainty that a supernatural interference has occurred;

"Given all the above, the canonical commission, set up by your Eminence, has considered these matters seriously and, having called on Almighty God for guidance, declares:

"1. That it considers the fact that Mlle Fretel was cured instantaneously, with no subsequent period of convalescence, and without the agency of any physical curative agent, to be certain;

"2. That the cause of the cure is to be attributed to a specific interference by Almighty God, through the intercession of Our Lady of Lourdes;

"3. That it is our unanimous verdict that your Eminence can, in consequence, safely pronounce the cure to be a miracle. Rennes, November 4th, 1950.

B. de Montgermont, titular canon (president)

A. Martin, vicar general (1st assessor)

F. Lauruelle, tit. can. (2nd assessor and secretary)

Jh. Anger, tit. can. (promoter of the faith)"

CHAPTER VIII

SCIENTIFICALLY EXTRAORDINARY CURES NOT YET CANONICALLY RECOGNISED

The File Procedure of the Lourdes Medical Bureau

THE following will give an idea of the method of filing information. On the cover of the dossier are written the full name, date of cure, etc., together with an index of the documents contained in the file, and inside there are at least six quarto sheets made up as follows:

Diocese of Tarbes and Lourdes

Diocesan Pilgrimage of..

from...................... *to*......................19.........

LOURDES MEDICAL BUREAU
Centre for Scientific Research

Year 19......

Surname and Christian names..

Date of birth ....

Profession ....

In hospital at ....

Examined at the ⎱ *First time* ....19......

Medical Bureau ⎰ *Second time* .... 19......

Diagnosis ....

....

....

FIRST EXAMINATION

Date of the examination.....................................19......
Carried out by Doctors..
....
....
Report drawn up by Doctor.................of......................
....
Patient's personal and family background...........................
....
....
....

MEDICAL HISTORY

....
....
....

HISTORY OF THE CURE—WITNESSES

....
....
....
Doctor .... of.......................
Full address..
is to furnish supplementary information.

SECOND EXAMINATION

Carried out on.....................................19.........
By Doctors ....
....
....

Report drawn up by Doctor.................. of....................

....

....

....

Doctors' Signatures:

1. *Did the disease described in the medical certificate or certificates certainly exist at the time of the pilgrimage to Lourdes?* ....

....

2. *Was the disease suddenly arrested in its progress at a moment when there was no reason to expect improvement?*

....

....

3. *Has there been a cure? Did it take place without medical treatment?* ....

....

....

4. *Are there any grounds for postponing judgments?*..............

....

....

5. *Is there any possible medical explanation of the cure?*.........

....

Does it exceed the laws of nature?................................

....

....

Lourdes,......................19......

Doctors' Signatures:

Further examinations made after the cure was recognised by the medical bureau...

....

....

Compilation of the Case Histories

The cures at Lourdes are "screened" by a whole series of organisations before they are published.

Immediately it is known that a cure has taken place, the medical bureau makes a preliminary examination and begins a file called the case history or dossier of the cure. Although the public, with their thirst for the sensational, would have it so, this file is in no sense a proof that there has been a miracle. It is no more than the very first step, the opening of an inquiry into the matter.

In the course of this first session, at which the subject of the alleged cure is present, such records of the case as have been brought with the pilgrimage are gone through; depositions are taken from the witnesses; the sick person is examined and every effort is made to establish his exact condition both before his arrival in Lourdes and on his appearance before the medical bureau.

One of the doctors is appointed secretary and the case is then put before the plenary session of the bureau, and every doctor present—we repeat, *every* doctor present, whatever his race, colour, religion or philosophy—is at perfect liberty to take what part he likes in the discussion. *That is the first stage.*

At the close of this meeting, either the case appears to warrant further investigation and is set aside until the following year, or it does not, and in that case it is immediately dropped.

If it is to be followed up the sick person is kept under observation and a local doctor is appointed as investigator. His task is to carry out this investigation during the year, collecting fresh documents and filling up any gaps there may be in the evidence of the witnesses, and to present the case once again at the end of the year, together with the fruits of his researches.

The so-called severity of the medical bureau is shown in all its rigour at this first stage. We have already indi-

L

cated how many reasons there are for caution. The following statistics will serve to illustrate this:

In 1946, thirty-six cases of alleged cures were retained for fuller investigation. Of these thirty-six only fourteen were re-examined in 1947, and no more than four passed the second examination.

In 1947, seventy-five cases were retained. Only eleven of these returned the following year, and six were accepted.

In 1948, eighty-three cases were accepted at the first inquiry, of which fifteen survived and only nine were submitted to the National Medical Council.

Each year, of course, several other cases were carried forward from one year to the next for further inquiry.

All this means that, whatever happens, no cure is ever given public recognition until two years, and sometimes more, have elapsed.

After the first examination the person whose case has been retained is asked to come back the following year. He is once more examined, studied, discussed at length, and at the end of this second examination the board decides whether or not to transmit the case to the National Medical Council of which we have spoken in Chapter VI. This council studies each case piecemeal, appointing a secretary who draws up a circumstantial and detailed report, weighing the pros and cons without emotion or partiality.

If the case seems sufficiently established and contains authentic proofs capable of carrying conviction it is transmitted to the canonical commissions of the Church for theological judgment.

The canonical commission is set up for each individual case by the bishop of the diocese. There is no permanent canonical commission. And it is by no means rare to find that cases which have been accepted on two distinct occasions in successive years by the medical bureau, and have passed the scrutiny of the National Medical Council with flying colours, fail to be accepted by the canonical commissions as miraculous. Far from seeing miracles everywhere, as many critics of the Church are fond of proclaiming, the canonical commissions are so strict in matters of principle, so careful in questions of detail, procedure and form, that when a case does succeed in passing through the sifting process we may be sure that it really is extraordinary and quite outside the laws of nature.

There are also cures that have appeared to doctors to be inexplicable, but on which the canonical commissions have as yet made no pronouncement or which they have set aside for various reasons, which we shall endeavour to describe. We outline below two of the numerous examples at our disposal.

GÉRARD BAILLIE

At the time of writing (1954), this child's case was still in the hands of the diocesan canonical commission. The case has been the subject of a considerable amount of heated argument both in the press and at the Lourdes Medical Bureau. The authors wish to make it clear that this account is included here simply as a scientific phenomenon and no dogmatic implication should be read into it.

Gérard Baillie (Saint-Pol-sur-Mer) developed bilateral choroiditis[1] at the age of just over two.

The disease consists of a progressive degeneration of the inner coats of the eye—the choroid and retina—and is believed to be of infective origin. Sight gradually fails as the parts responsible for vision become affected, the fields of vision decreasing until the site of entry of the optic nerve (the fundus oculi) itself becomes atrophic. Blindness results and is incurable.

In this child's case the earliest symptoms of disease became apparent after he had had a general anaesthetic for the surgical treatment of a hernia; by the age of two and a half he was blind. He was admitted to the Institute for the Blind, Arras. Dr (Mme) Biziaut, ophthalmologist of Dunkirk, had certified that the child was suffering from bilateral optic atrophy and incurable blindness (the latter words underlined).

The child stayed at the institute for two years. No one among the teachers, prefects or lady superintendent of the place raised any objection to the diagnosis of blindness. Furthermore, Dr Viton, ophthalmologist of Arras, made a note on the child's house record as follows: "Bilateral choroiditis. Bilateral optic atrophy. Incurable blindness."

The child came to Lourdes at the age of four and a half after he had been in the institute for two years. There several doctors saw him. They, and others with the child, noted the fact of his blindness. It seems unlikely, moreover, that a child aged four and a half could successfully simulate blindness for two years without being detected. He conscientiously undertook the usual pilgrimage practices at Lourdes and on the fourth day there the following event took place:

Between the third and fourth stations of the way of the Cross, where his mother had taken him (the path is steep and rather rough), the child's vision returned.

He saw his mother and with all the loving simplicity of which a child is capable said, "Mummy, what a pretty dress you've got." He saw his mother as though through a slit—an important piece of evidence—and it seemed as if the curtains which had closed some two years previously were now slowly opening. The child himself seems to have become explicitly aware a good deal later of the fact that his sight had returned. He was seen at the medical bureau that same evening. (One author [F.L.] was present at this examination.) The child could certainly see, but in an unusual way. It seemed as if he was seeing down two tubes, which apparently prevented him from enjoying "whole" vision. He also seemed unable to see things in perspective. He was able to take a watch into his hands and point out things close to him.

By next day he could see very well and his whole visual field had apparently returned to normal. He was able to leap from bed to bed in the dormitory of the Seven Dolours Hospital. He went into the lift and played with all the buttons. He was taken to see a reputable ophthalmologist (Dr Camps, of Tarbet) by Dr Leuret. Dr Camps had been a student at France's premier school of ophthalmology in Paris and his evidence cannot be lightly set aside. The latter, in a rather sceptical frame of mind, examined the child conscientiously and for a long time. He concluded by saying that the boy had bilateral choroiditis and optic atrophy. "He should be unable to see." Yet the child could see, though apparently as if through a coarse mesh.

On the return journey to Lourdes the child was treated (almost deliberately on God's part, it seemed) to a striking view of the snow-flecked mountains lit up by the rays of the rising sun. He was thrilled and full of questions. It all had to be explained to him.

The child left Lourdes and returned to the Institute for the Blind. Here, despite the fact that no one had apparently noticed this in the two years previous to this event, it was soon spotted that he could see, and at the lady superintendent's request, his parents removed him to Saint John-Baptist's School, Dunkirk. Since then the child has attended this ordinary school and has walked there by himself every day, crossing several main streets on the way. It should be noted that his home is about two miles from the school and his return journey is made at dusk—a notoriously bad time for those whose vision is defective.

The child's school progress is normal and he takes part in the three R's. Specimens of his school notebooks are included in his case records. He can read writing on the blackboard. He behaves like a person with normal vision, though the last recorded examination credits him with a visual acuity of 0·2/0·3.

The child was seen the following year by Dr Smith (ophthalmologist, of Glasgow) who after careful examination confirmed the diagnosis of Dr Camps made the year before. "The child has bilateral choroiditis and optic atrophy. He should not be able to see."

He was able to copy a series of letters which had been noiselessly written down on a sheet of white paper. He could do simple sums such as boys of his age should be able to do. He could do subtraction and addition where the only indication was a plus or minus sign. He was able unhesitatingly to pick out a given object, a pencil, knife, watch or bell, from among a number of things scattered on a table. He was able to pick out the red cross in the badge of members of the medical bureau.

The case will no doubt give rise to further discussion. Some doctors have expressed surprise that Our Lady should only have partially restored the child's vision. The remark has been made that Our Lady should have restored one hundred per cent vision to the child. It seems difficult to see how one can dictate to Our Lady in these matters. She seems to act as she thinks fit, not as we would wish her to.

In 1947-48 the medical bureau passed the documents to the National Medical Commission for further assessment, in view of the contradictory arguments which had taken place at Lourdes. This body decided to have the child examined again. The child went to see Dr Lescaut, ophthalmologist, of Lille, ophthalmic surgeon to the hospitals of that city. The result of his examination was unexpected.

"There can be no reasonable doubt that Gérard Baillie had choroiditis and optic atrophy in both eyes. However, he has neither of these now. I have never come across a case in which bilateral choroiditis with optic atrophy has been cured."

Here then are two consecutive pieces of information, each quite out of the ordinary.

A child can apparently see for two years, during which time his visual equipment is apparently not functioning. (One might compare the situation in which a camera took photographs without films.)

No record is known to us of the "reconstruction" of a retina and optic nerve which had been non-functioning for two years. Vision damaged by the effects of cerebral tumours can return if the tumour is dealt with early enough, if the optic atrophy has lasted for three or four months, but we have no knowledge of this happening when the atrophy has lasted two years. This is particularly so if the latter is the result of choroiditis.[2]

This case strikingly illustrates the point already made: Our Lady seems to act as though she wished for medical inquiry into her activities. Over a period of two years all medical records available indicate that Gérard Baillie was a victim of bilateral choroiditis and optic atrophy. When this fact had been firmly established the child was completely cured.[3]

MME GESTAS

Professor Pierre Mauriac's Report

"I saw Mme Gestas again on February 10th, 1951. She weighed 149 pounds, was rather overweight, but claimed to be in excellent health though troubled with mild vascular symptoms referable to the menopause.

"Clinical examination was quite negative. Abdominal examinations revealed no tenderness or thickening, there is no evidence of any disturbance of function of the alimentary tract. She has seen no doctor for over a year, except for a bout of diarrhœa in September last. She leads an active life, never complains of stomach trouble, rides a bicycle, but considers herself too stout. She is married, has a healthy son. Up to the age of twenty-five she was subject to attacks of breathlessness.

"In December, 1943, she underwent a gastrectomy for an ulcer of the lesser curvature. However, gastric symptoms persisted and Dr Dubarry performed a second laparotomy for a small diaphragmatic hernia (the stomach had herniated through the oesophageal opening) on May 11th, 1944. In the course of this operation part of the transverse colon was removed because of some evidence of inflammation around that organ.

"The patient recovered from the operation in three weeks. On her return home, however, symptoms suggestive of peritonitis developed; she ran a temperature, and was in bed for eighteen days while ice bags were applied. She never seemed to improve after getting up. She could do no work for a year, needed to rest several times a day and had to get a servant to help her in the house.

"An X-ray taken in November, 1945, revealed another diaphragmatic hernia and at the patient's request a third laparotomy was done on January 4th, 1946. The viscera in the epigastrium were found to be involved in thick adhesions. The operation was prolonged and its sequelae serious—the patient was in shock, developed pulmonary congestion, and a fistula formed which lasted several months.

"The patient spent a month in the clinic and then returned home to bed for a further two months. When she got up she continued to suffer from dyspeptic symptoms, vomiting and abdominal pains, similar to those found in ulceration of the alimentary tract; she also suffered from intermittent attacks of intestinal obstruction sometimes associated with fecal vomiting. One such attack required continuous aspiration for forty-eight hours.

"A fourth laparotomy was considered, but conservative treatment was decided upon. Mme Gestas was now very exhausted and weighed only 99 pounds (normal weight 146 pounds). She was at this point persuaded by a cousin to go to Lourdes.

"She states that she came back from Lourdes unimproved. However, Dr Dubourg, her surgeon, noted that the attacks of intestinal obstruction became less and that Mme Gestas had put on several pounds in weight. He recorded, however, that she continued to suffer from painful attacks which suggested that the peritonitis was still active in the subumbilical region. Her general health, he considered, though improved, remained poor.

"Mme Gestas remained subject to such discomfort as to prevent any active life on her part; she continued to suffer from attacks of partial obstruction and abdominal pains. In an attempt to relieve the latter, Dr Dubourg tried injections about the sympathetic nervous system. The treatment was unsuccessful. So the patient's life dragged wearily on until August, 1947.

"On the 21st of that month she set off once more for Lourdes. On her first visit water had simply been poured over her; on this occasion (August 22nd, 1947) she underwent a complete bath. She immediately felt a tearing sensation throughout her abdominal viscera; that afternoon she wondered (rather doubtfully) whether the pains were less. She awoke the following Saturday with no discomfort and, abandoning all her dietetic precautions, she ate string beans which she digested painlessly.

"Since then Mme Gestas has had no further functional or painful symptoms referable to her abdomen and has put on forty-eight pounds in weight. We may summarise the case as follows:

"The patient, aged fifty, underwent three laparotomies—for gastric ulcer and inflammation and adhesions about the colon. She was suddenly cured after bathing at Lourdes. As a result she was freed of all alimentary symptoms which had prevented her working for several years and which had brought about a loss of forty-eight pounds. Mme Gestas is, at this writing, in excellent health.

"Having dealt with the medical aspects of the case, I should like to draw attention to certain features which might prove of interest to Catholic doctors.

"Mme Gestas had been a non-practising Catholic from the age of twenty, despite the fact that she was baptised and made her first Holy Communion. She has been married once, divorced and married again. While in hospital for her second operation, the nun in charge of Mme Gestas suggested that she should be married in the presence of a priest. Her first husband was now dead. This ceremony was carried through with the consent of both parties, at Mme Gestas' home, by a Capuchin father.

"The above event did not result in any change of attitude

on her part toward the practice of her religion; she went to Lourdes under the influence of some pressure she was unable to account for. At Lourdes she refused to be bathed, but allowed herself to be sprinkled with water. She states that on her return home, though physically no better, her 'soul was cured and she began to pray.'

"By the time she went on a second pilgrimage her faith had gradually returned. Her husband, almost anti-religious, went with her and witnessed her cure which impressed him considerably, but he denied its miraculous nature. He pointed out to his wife that the religious authorities did not consider it miraculous either.

"Mme Gestas is, at the time of writing, a Franciscan tertiary; she strikes me as calm and unexcitable; she gives no evidence of functional nervous unbalance despite the fact that she is menopausal. She wants her cure officially recognised as miraculous because she hopes this may convert her husband.

"Last year I wrote: 'This cure must await confirmation by the passage of time. Then the part played by the organic lesions and by the nervous unbalance in the production of her symptoms will need to be discussed.'

"Time has confirmed the cure. I find myself in a quandary when it comes to discussing the part played by the organic lesions and the nervous unbalance.[4] I have seen (or rather the surgeon has) the organic lesions. But I can detect no signs or symptoms referable to nervous unbalance. If they ever existed they have been cured along with the organic lesions which troubled the patient so much for four years.

"This case, which last year I could not see my way to confirming as outside of nature's laws, I now feel cannot be considered as within its bounds."

CHAPTER IX

AN UNUSUAL CURE

*Interesting from the medical point of view, but providing
no direct proof of supernatural intervention*

MANY cases of this kind could be recorded in this chapter. One has been chosen to illustrate the point that cures can occur which are difficult to account for in orthodox medical terms, yet for which evidence of supernatural intervention is lacking.

DANIEL KYLMETIS (1947)
*(Pott's disease with abscess formation and evidence of
spinal cord compression)*

At the age of seven this child developed Pott's disease in the cervical region. The sixth and seventh cervical vertebrae collapsed and the first thoracic vertebra was infected.

The child was surgically immobilised. Owing to the neck rigidity it was not possible to alter the position of his head. An abscess arising in the affected bones had burrowed its way into the mediastinum which resulted in great difficulty in swallowing. Signs of cord compression were also present (probably due to a pachymeningitis) giving rise to painful micturition and sphincter disturbances.

In September, 1947, the child came to Lourdes on pilgrimage. His condition improved suddenly and showed the following characteristics: The painful difficulty in swallowing vanished instantaneously, as did the pain on passing water. The neck rigidity became less over a period of days and the ability to move the head returned. The child was seen again at the Bureau of

Scientific Studies in September, 1948. A note of this examination follows:

"Daniel Kylmetis, Grenoble, France. Examined September 13th, 1948.
"General condition: the child is emaciated.
"Heart rate: 88 per minute.
"Heart: no abnormalities of sounds or in rhythm detected. No additional sounds heard.
"Lungs: no abnormal signs elicited.
"Vertebral column: no evidence of abscess arising from bony structures. The head can be easily moved in any direction. Pressure on the bony parts of the spinal column in all regions (with the child in the sitting position) is painless. The child could be placed in a position of forced flexion without producing evidence of any spinal column rigidity.
"The inguinal and femoral zones of the lower limbs included some enlarged glands. Active and passive movements of the lower limbs normal. Sensation normal. Cutaneous and deep reflexes normal.
"Upper limbs: normal movements, sensation and reflexes.
"Babinski's sign was not elicited.
"The child can walk rather unsteadily and jerkily without his surgical appliance. (This is his first attempt at doing without the latter.)"

After this examination Dr Mollaret (with Dr Champeau's help) drew up the following statement, presented in the form of an address to the assembled doctors.

"Your excellency, Mr President, ladies and gentlemen. It is my task to bring to your attention an interesting though unspectacular case. Let me explain that I have only had this child under my care for forty-eight hours; I first took charge of him when he joined the Dauphinois pilgrimage. I am neither the doctor who usually treats him nor otherwise responsible for him. All I know of him is contained in a certificate issued by Dr Cadoz, of Grenoble, who has looked after him since 1944. This document has been put in the patient's file this morning. I have also this morning been given, by the child's mother, X-ray photographs taken at intervals since 1944 (which you will see in a moment) which have, since 1945, made it possible to make a firm diagnosis of Pott's disease involving the fifth, sixth, and seventh cervical vertebrae.

"For the eight months after its birth in 1941, the child was considered poorly. After delivery he developed pylorospasm and suffered from an angioma. He was always delicate and walked at the age of seventeen months.

"At the age of three (in 1944) he slid down the banisters in such a way as to twist himself and apparently did himself some internal damage. His neck was not evidently injured. Shortly after this a diagnosis of cervical tuberculosis involving cervical vertebrae five, six and seven was suggested, the illness starting in 1944 and the diagnosis being confirmed in 1945. In 1946 signs of an abscess developed, with evidence of mediastinal and cord involvement. Dysphagia, painful micturition and muscle spasm were noted. Both plantar reflexes were extensor. By 1947 the child was seriously ill and the attending physician considered the child incurable and death only a little time away. The child came to Lourdes in September, 1947.

"After his return to Grenoble his mother was pleasantly surprised to find that the child's condition had improved over a period of days, and the doctor in charge of the case noted the progressive disappearance of the signs of cord compression. (Plaster of Paris casing was taken off in July, 1948). The surgical frame was removed and a lighter piece of equipment fitted. The child, who had stopped walking in 1944, was now able to stand alone and take some hesitant steps. The dysphagia disappeared. From being able to micturate painfully once daily in 1947 the child could now pass water easily and painlessly; the abscess could no longer be easily seen.

"Discussion. This is an example of the sort of case occasionally recorded, in which anatomical lesions apparently unimproved are associated with functional cure. X-ray photographs taken in 1947 and 1949, i.e., before and after 'cure,' indicate that no change has taken place in the bones involved.

"However, despite the radiological persistence of the bony lesions, there can be no doubt that the child, who is not suspected of hysteria or malingering, had suddenly recovered the ability to move his vertebral column; nor could any tenderness or rigidity be detected even on forced flexion of the head."

The above report was brought to the attention of Dr Sorrel. He stated: "It is an unusual case, but it could occur naturally."

Following the above report the whole matter was put before the National Medical Commission.

The case raises points of medico-philosophic interest, illustrating as it does the apparent divorce between signs and symptoms and pathological lesions.

In 1949 the following report was received from the doctor in charge of the case:

"I saw this interesting little boy last week, just before the beginning of the holidays—during which he plans to go to Lourdes. He is very well indeed. His plaster of Paris casing is off as is his light surgical appliance. The latest X-rays are satisfactory. He walks well, his legs are strong and his schooling continues satisfactorily. Last winter he suffered from measles and scarlet fever, without sequelae. He eats well and is full of energy. I consider him as being cured and am impressed by the rate of improvement.

(Signed) Dr E. Cadoz."

CHAPTER X

ETIOLOGY AND PHYSIOLOGY OF MIRACULOUS CURES[1]

WE have seen, with the help of typical cases, how the *diagnosis* of a miraculous cure is arrived at both from the scientific and the theological point of view. Science says that a natural cure was impossible in the conditions under which the disease existed; the patient, the public and the doctor all agree that there was a probability of divine intervention; the Church confirms this assumption in certain of the cases submitted to her judgment, without, however, denying the possibility of divine intervention in others because of her rejection of them.[2]

The paramount consideration from the scientific standpoint is the impossibility of a cure by natural means. This is really the fundamental problem, and in general it is this problem on which doctors and theologians concentrate their attention. We have seen how satisfactorily it is dealt with in the light of modern science.

But that does not mean that a satisfactory answer has been found for every problem raised by miraculous cures.

Doctor Le Bec shows the way to be followed in his masterly work *Les Preuves médicales du Miracle* when he deals with what he calls the "Physiology of the Supernatural" and attempts to analyse the inner workings of a miraculous cure. No doubt some will raise the objections once made by a medical man: "How is tuberculosis cured at Lourdes? We have no idea, and I shall certainly not try to explain the mysterious mechanism of the cure, for if we understood that, there would be nothing supernatural left."

This is a fundamental error. As the book of Genesis tells us, the world was given to us for our use.[3] That is why we have been endowed with intelligence, and we have the right and the duty to push our study of nature to its uttermost limits, for it is thus that we shall find God. The Israelite host bowed their heads to the dust when God passed by . . . and then went off and adored the golden calf; Moses himself went up toward the burning bush to see why it did not burn away, and there he met God face to face.

It is our right also to find out why the burning bush is not consumed; why in spite of infection, destruction of tissue and deep-seated lesions, disease is wiped out in defiance of all human probability.

The Church expects the scientist to assure her that the operation of natural causes was quite incapable of giving an adequate explanation of the extraordinary fact under review.[4]

The scientist is therefore bound to examine all the known laws of nature which might have brought some influence to bear on the phenomenon.

Having learned with Laënnec to connect certain lesions with certain results of auscultation, the doctor cannot reply to the Church's question without using auscultation and discussing the existence, non-existence or disappearance of the lesions. Having learned with Pasteur of the existence and part played by microbes in disease, the doctor may not leave them out of account in his examination of a cure, and neglect to test a case of tuberculosis for Koch's bacilli. Having discovered with Roentgen the possibilities of investigations by X-rays, the Church requires that he include the results of radiological examinations in his case histories. Having learned with modern physicists of the atomic and dynamic constitution of matter, the doctor cannot afford to leave the fresh data thus supplied out of his calculations. The Church demands that the scientist pursue his researches as far as his science will permit, and refuses to allow the possibility of a miracle until he is ready to say: "We have looked everywhere and done everything, and not only is there no possible explanation of the case, but it is in flat contradiction to the conditions which alone are relevant to it." The Church sets no bounds to the researches of the scientist.

Let us therefore face squarely the problem of the *etiology* and *physiology* of miraculous cures. Three reservations must be made at the outset:

1. In our study we shall class under one heading cures officially recognised as miraculous and those which may be scientifically presumed such. From the standpoint of biology they are indistinguishable. In this we follow the example of the Hamburg biologist von Uexküll, who found that he could not even begin his work without the presupposition of a divine plan, for we too can do nothing with the second class of cures without presupposing divine intervention.

2. Apart from this hypothesis which at least has the merit of being founded on an analogy of the facts, we shall hazard a number of others. It is the function of science to start from facts and build up hypotheses, the proving or disproving of which will extend or define the field of our knowledge. Our hypotheses should therefore be for the reader, as for us, mere aids to work and thought, nothing more.

3. This book forms part of a collection, the purpose of which is to study biological facts in the light of Catholic doctrine.[5] Hence we cannot avoid trespassing on the realm of theology as well as that of medicine. As we have already stated, we have no doctrinal intent, but desire only to give a personal survey of the subject.

It may seem strange to talk about *etiology*, the science of causes, when dealing with miraculous or presumably miraculous cures. Is not God by definition the cause of all miracles? That is true, but we saw in our first chapter how God's use of secondary causes, of natural agents, even in the greatest of miracles, is set down in black and

M

white in the Bible: the wind which divided the Red Sea, the likelihood of a fall of aerolites, of optical refraction, of multiplication of substance by means of an existing nucleus, etc.

On the other hand theology and common sense demand that if God disrupts the normal order of things, it should be strictly within the limits of the purpose He has in mind: thus in a private cure, worked purely for the good of the individual, His intervention may well pass unnoticed; if the spiritual good of a large number of people is intended, it may be more spectacular. Between these two extremes there is a whole series, ranging from the grace which sets in motion a natural chain of cause and effect in someone's favour to divine intervention manifested in the flagrant and multiple violation of nature's laws.[6]

We shall therefore be led to distinguish what belongs to the direct action of the first cause and what belongs to His use of intermediaries in the cures under consideration.

Let us repeat that a miracle is not worked by waving a magic wand; it is not something fantastic and irrational; it is an action of the Supreme Intelligence, of Almighty Power, with a definite end in view and using logical means to attain it.

In accordance with the classification proposed in 1936 by Abbé Journet, professor of the University of Fribourg, divine intervention in the human body may follow one of two main lines: either diapsychological action (using the soul) or parapsychological action (by-passing the soul).[7]

Thus in a case of infectious disease divine intervention may either vitalise the soul, the life-principle, to an unprecedented degree, so that the organism becomes capable of overcoming a normally incurable disease (diapsychological action) or else destroy the microbe directly, stimulate the production of antibodies and antitoxins, of bacteriophages, and restore the tissues to their former integrity (parapsychological action).

Since we cannot overlook the possibility of creative and miraculous action in the purely spiritual order, we may conclude that the human being may be the object of God's extraordinary intervention in four ways: spiritual action, creative action, diapsychological action and parapsychological action.

With *spiritual action* (revelations, visions and the like) we are not at present concerned. *Creative action* in the sense of creation *ex nihilo* does not seem to be indicated, since even when God created man He used an already existing substance, the slime of the earth. Hence the repair of the human frame must apparently be reduced to a relative creation with the help of existing materials, and that brings us back to the field of parapsychological action.

Diapsychological action seems capable of existing in three forms:

1. *Spiritual action:* for example, a conversion such as that described in Chapter III. We have already made some reservations with regard to the purely spiritual nature of conversions, but it is clearly a possibility.

2. *Psychological action:* influencing both the spiritual and somatic factors in the development of a person's thought.

The bodily factors might be set in motion either by diapsychological action of the sort we shall discuss presently or by parapsychological action. We are not yet in a position to test such a theory, but it may be that neurology, experimental and comparative psychology will remedy this in the near future.

The numerous conversions recorded at the various sanctuaries may well be the effect either of ordinary divine action on the conscience or of an extraordinary action along the spiritual or psychological lines just mentioned.

Moreover the sensation of well-being, of perfect health, the psychological reawakening which are so often associated with miraculous cures may belong to this category.

3. *Diapsychological action* properly so called: The human soul, the vital principle, created by God, deriving its power from God, could be activated in an extraordinary way so that the vital processes were raised to a degree never observed in normal biology, far beyond the uttermost imaginable limits of artificial or therapeutic stimulation.

In this respect the hypothesis seems to be quite definitely supported by the facts. We have only to re-read what has been written here to see invalids, bedridden for months and even years, do what the paralytic did in the Gospel, take up their bed and walk. Ankylosis, contraction of the tendons, weakness of atrophied muscles, glandular and other inactivity are overcome or remedied in an instant, so that the normal course of life can be resumed at once or after a very short delay. The organism is transformed at a moment's notice by the recovery of its functions and activity in a manner which seems to point inexorably to an extraordinary activation of the vital principle.

This must surely have been the case in the cure of Mlle Jeanne Fretel (which was in all probability due to a combination of diapsychological and parapsychological action, for God is not bound by our classifications!) as far as the improvement in her general health was concerned. One of us who has for thirty years directed a clinic for diseases of the digestive and nutritive organs, and has treated many hundreds of emaciated patients, has never seen a gain of thirty-one pounds in sixteen days. He has observed gains of eleven to thirteen pounds in the course of the first or second week of treatment through rehydration of the system in patients who have excessively restricted their drinking or have been subject to repeated vomiting. But in the following weeks the maximum rate of increase was about four to five pounds weekly, and both patient and doctor were delighted even with that. Indeed, to obtain even these results it was usually necessary to keep the patient in bed so as to avoid any exertion and loss of weight. That did not happen in Mlle Fretel's case.

Her increase in weight, re-hydration included (her doctor reported that she took only small quantities of liquid) was almost twenty-four pounds in the first seven days and a further seven and a half pounds in the next nine days. That indicates that the process of assimilation was intensified to an abnormal degree and seems to point to its being the secondary effect of an extraordinary activation of the vital principle.[8]

This process may be used to explain the cures of more or less localised lesions which do not take place instantaneously in the strict sense, but over a certain period—and we shall see later that such cases are not infrequent.

Finally this intensification of the vital functions may be such as to stimulate the production of enormous quantities of antitoxins and antibodies, sterilising and disinfecting an organism suffering from a microbial disease almost instantaneously or very rapidly, for example, the negativation of the skin reaction as in the Hébert case.[9]

Parapsychological action is suggested by those instantaneous or practically instantaneous cures which apparently leave no room for the operation of physiological processes, even raised to an unprecedented degree. Its presence may perhaps be presumed in the following cases:

Instantaneous replacement of tissue: M. Auguste Aerts was operated on in Antwerp on June 21st, 1927, for acute non-calculous cholecystitis, probably due to B. coli. In consequence a fistula developed, discharging pus and bile, which, if accidentally obstructed, caused attacks of extreme pain, culminating in an abundant flow of purulent and bilious matter. He set out for Lourdes on June 18th, 1928, without much conviction, but in deference to his family's wishes. His dressings had to be renewed several times on the way. On his arrival next day the doctors found that not only was the dressing quite saturated with pus, but the bandage and even his shirt as well. On June 20th the attendants who bathed him saw that dressings and shirt were again soaked with pus. On the 21st the dressing contained no liquid matter whatever, and was as clean as when it had been put on the previous evening. At the medical bureau, examination showed that the orifice of the fistula was completely covered with healthy skin, without any sign of a break.[10]

The fact that the dressing, placed over a fully active fistula the day before, was not soiled at all indicates an immediate closing of the wound; the fact that this did not cause the usual concomitants of retention indicates that the bile ducts were also cleared without delay; and the fact that healthy skin was observed the next day implies an ultra-rapid replacement of the tissues.

The instantaneousness and simultaneity of local curative effects suggest the direct local action of an external agent, and perhaps the presence of other factors, of which we shall speak in a moment.

Disappearance of substance: In the cases of Mme Acar (Chapter III), Mme Martin (Chapter VII) and Mme Augault, who suffered from a fibroma as big as a man's head, which on August 21st, 1926, after a bath in the piscine, was reduced to the size of a fist,[11] we find the instantaneous or very rapid reabsorption of tumours without the toxic accidents (whether uræmic or otherwise) which are often found in the infinitely less rapid reabsorption effected by radium or X-ray treatment.

A miraculous cure recognised as such by the archbishop of Rennes gives us the opportunity of proposing a bold, perhaps even a rash theory to explain these cases. We crave forgiveness—we are only exploring.

Sister Marie-Marguerite, born on April 13th, 1872, a religious in the Poor Clare Convent of Rennes, as a result of troubles of a cardiac and renal nature, spread over the years 1924-1934, was suffering from suppurating nephritis which, coupled with complications due to cardiac failure, in 1936 developed generalised œdema, particularly in the legs where bullae formed, burst and began to discharge serum constantly. Cardiac dyspnœa made it impossible for her to stay in bed, and the patient had to remain seated in an armchair day and night.

On January 20th, 1937, the community began a novena to Our Lady of Lourdes to beg for a cure. "On January 22nd, 1937," writes Dr Philouze, the doctor in charge of the case, "at eight o'clock in the morning, the patient dragged herself painfully to the chapel adjoining her sick room in order to assist at Mass. At the moment of the Elevation she suddenly had a feeling of compression all over her body, especially in her legs, where the swellings seemed to subside instantaneously; the bandages round them fell to the floor of their own accord. As soon as Mass was over the patient returned to her room without any difficulty and found that the œdema had completely vanished. She put on her slippers, which she had been unable to wear for more than a year, went downstairs and walked about the house all day without feeling any fatigue and without any sign of a heart attack."[12]

In November, 1945, at the request of the archbishop of Rennes, a medical commission composed of Drs Regnault, Paul Hardoin and Lanchou examined Sister Marie-Marguerite, then seventy-three years of age, and could only report that she was in excellent health: her heart was normal, her kidneys neither palpable nor painful, and there was no œdema. They concluded that the cure could not be explained by natural causes.

In this cure one essential peculiarity must be noted: the disappearance of the œdema was instantaneous,[13] and the bandages dropped to the ground. What happened to the fluid, of which there must certainly have been at least several quarts? For it is known that œdema of up to three pints may remain imperceptible, and hers was all too obvious!

She thought at first that the œdema must have drained away through the wounds in her legs and formed a "pool" at her feet. But we have personally received an assurance that there was not a drop of water on the ground, and that her dressings were dry and clean. Hence the water was not drained off externally in liquid form. On the other hand, there was no abnormal passing of urine, either in quantity or in frequency. In any case, where could this water have been retained, after it had suddenly disappeared from the tissues where it had lain, until such time as it could be passed as urine?

Only cutaneous and pulmonary evaporation remain. But the normal pulmonary fluid loss is not more than $\frac{1}{2}$-$\frac{7}{8}$ pint in twenty-four hours, and that from the skin about the same. To get rid of a quart in one hour, the circulation of the blood as well as the respiratory movements would have to be greatly accelerated, and above all the renewal of the air at the body's surface and at the pulmonary alveoli would have to be twenty-four times as rapid . . . and for a gallon . . . there is no need to push the hypothesis any further. It becomes absurd.

But what did happen to the water?

What about a parapsychological action producing a local perspiration with immediate evaporation? But that would inevitably have meant that the limb would have been frozen stiff. The evaporation of quite small quantities of water is enough to freeze a whole jugful.[14]

To suggest the complete and absolute annihilation of the water *in situ* brings us dangerously close to the magician's wand, and attributes to God an alternately creative and destructive activity quite foreign to what we know of Him. For God did not even annihilate Lucifer or Judas.

We have therefore to widen our horizons, to look at the matter from God's level, to consider higher physical levels than those with which we are familiar.

Let us briefly recall the principles: we are able to make a

rough distinction between the subatomic world, ruled by the relations between the particles constituting, or capable of constituting, the atom; the atomic world which can be represented by stars still in the gaseous state, in which elementary mutations predominate; the mineral world (liquid or solidified stars) in which the atoms coalesce into molecules; the vegetable world built up on the mineral molecules; and the animal world which can only use molecules of organic substance produced by the vegetable world. But the more complex superior orders have at least some of their activities in common with the inferior.

What happens within the tissue itself? There are of course molecules of albumin, fat and sugar, but in their mutations there are many other atoms which they transform: dialysis through the capillary and cell walls can carry quite sizable molecules, so there is no reason why atoms should not pass the same way.

If therefore we find that the disappearance of the œdema cannot be explained by vascular and pulmonary activity because the circulatory and respiratory systems are unable to cope with it; if we find the perspiration theory ruled out by the impossibility of the capillaries allowing a sufficiently rapid outlet to the sweat glands and by the freezing caused by cutaneous evaporation, we must have recourse to an external dispersal of the liquid and of the substances in solution (urea, salts, etc.) without the help of the circulatory system.

We must fall back on dialysis through the walls and interstices of all the cells separating each molecule of water inside the limb from the outside surface of the skin. That is not impossible since this sort of dialysis occurs in the phenomena of cellular assimilation and elimination, and it is bound to happen in multicellular non-vascular organisms.

The process is therefore possible, but if it is to be efficacious in this particular instance, it must be carried to an incommensurable degree: and surely this degree is just as impossible as the pulmonary hypothesis? Besides, the same problem arises regarding exit through the skin—there must be either perspiration (which there was not) or instantaneous evaporation causing intense cold, thereby freezing the limb.

It would seem that we must look elsewhere for a method of getting rid of the water, urea and salts constituting the œdema, one which will not be subject to the drawbacks of normal physiological mechanics, even when intensified *ad infinitum*.

We have already examined a similar problem when discussing the quality of *subtlety* which the human body will enjoy after its resurrection.[15] We have seen that modern physics rejects the continuity of matter. There are only infinitesimal particles of matter in perpetual movement, separated by immense "empty spaces." The cohesion of these particles into atoms, of atoms into molecules, of molecules into gases, liquids and solids is only achieved by a series of electrical forces. And the reason why bodies are not constantly passing through each other is that the network of forces which keeps the elements of one body together sets up an impenetrable barrier to the network of others.

Nevertheless atomic physics has revealed the presence of neutrons, impervious to the forces of these networks and capable of passing through them without difficulty. This of course is the ABC of nuclear physics and atomic piles.

Historically we know that the body of the risen Christ (image of our own resurrection, according to St Paul) passed through the closed doors of the upper room. This body was the same body which had been placed in the tomb. It could be touched, as Our Lord demonstrated to doubting Thomas, and could eat and drink, for Our Lord did so to show His apostles that He was not a ghost.

These facts were checked for us by St Thomas and the apostles, and we can put them to the additional test of our modern scientific knowledge—Our Lord's body was physically capable of passing through locked doors provided the constituent elements of His body were neutralised or their network of forces modified in such a manner as to do away with the opposition or resistance of the substance through which He had to pass.

The theories of modern physics, its experimental achievements, and the historical fact of the upper room all combine to prove the physical possibility of one substance passing through another without any reaction on either side; and it is likely that the peculiar condition of the substance at that moment would render it exempt from certain other natural laws, such as that governing the normal vaporisation of water with its consequences.[16]

We thus arrive at the point at which the divine action is applied to matter (for diapsychological action has had to be ruled out in this case), not at any level of organic substance but at the level of the very constituent forces of matter.

The hypothesis that several pints of water and other substances could be dispersed by this sort of action on the part of the Creator, by Whom everything exists and is maintained, is not unpleasing, especially if we think of the enormous factories required to produce a few tiny neutrons.

We may therefore wonder whether recourse may be had to some such explanation of the instantaneous or almost instantaneous disappearance of tumours, of which we have spoken.

Production of substance: An identical, but inverse problem is raised by the production of substance, such as the formation of callus in the famous case of Peter de Rudder. Dr Reverchon, professor of the Catholic University of Lille, has made a very thorough medico-surgical study of this case.[17] There was a compound traumatic fracture of both bones in the upper third of the left leg, sustained in 1867. There was a great deal of suppuration, containing fragments of necrosed bone and very pronounced pseudoarthrosis. By 1875 there was only one possible remedy, amputation. On April 7th, 1875, Peter de Rudder went to the chapel of Our Lady of Lourdes at Oostacker, near Ghent. He was suffering intensely, and had to rest on a bench. Then, under a sudden impulse, he got up, forgetting his crutches, went forward and knelt before the statue of Our Lady. Then he realised with amazement what had happened. He walked three times round the grotto. He was cured! He was examined at once. "The leg and foot which had been badly swollen a moment or two before had now returned to their normal size. The plaster cast and bandages which had been round them had fallen off. Both wounds were cicatrised and the broken bones had been suddenly joined together again."

There is a certain looseness of expression in that: if the bones had been "joined together again," in view of the considerable loss of substance through suppuration and elimination of sequestra, the leg would have been shortened, and it was not. As the post-mortem examination was to show later there had been an instantaneous formation of callus, filling the gap between the broken ends of the bone.

We are immediately faced with the problem: whence did the bone substance come, in particular the necessary salts of calcium required to harden it immediately?

Dr. Le Bec has very ably demonstrated that taking into account the quantity of calcium needed, the amount of salts of calcium in the bloodstream, the speed of circulation of the blood through its capillaries and the density of these last at the seat of the fracture, at least fifty days would be required for the formation of the callus by normal means. We are here in the presence of the same sort of material impossibility as in the case of the disappearance of Sister Marie-Marguerite's œdema.

In addition, the radiographs of the bones, taken by Dr Glorieux, show that Peter de Rudder's callus has none of the trabecular aspect of bones formed by the normal processes of ossification. Dr Reverchon concludes that this absence of trabeculation can "only be explained by an abnormal and rapid process of consolidation, an immense deposit of calcium in the form of an intermediary piece of bone, formed of interfragmentary mastic."

Here again, the only difficulty was that the necessary calcium was not present in the fluids round the wound, and could not have been brought there instantaneously.

We must therefore conclude that the calcium salts were brought to the spot, not by means of the circulatory system nor in molecular form, but by other means. That seems to indicate either a formation of calcium *in situ*, perhaps derived from the disintegrated elements of the œdema which had disappeared, or else a deposit of calcium from outside, penetrating into the tissues in atomic or subatomic form.

Let us bring our theory to a close with a question mark (one more or less matters little!). It is suggested by something we have already said about the multiplication of substance (Chapter I), namely the possible power of crystallisation of a certain initial quantity of substance. Is it possible that the ends of the bones at the seat of the fracture and the tissues round the wound could have exercised such an influence on elements brought in from outside?[18]

Correction of Deformities: The almost instantaneous correction of the rachitic deformities of young John O'Grady (Chapter III) sets us a very complex problem. It is understandable that rickety bowlegs should straighten slightly as the child grows, owing to the intensity of metabolic activity in childhood, and this is often the case. But it is difficult to conceive how this straightening process could take place there and then without any corresponding lengthening of the bone. To suggest that the bones became malleable and were straightened in consequence would be to depart yet further from normal processes.

Nevertheless the pain and muscular contraction accompanying the cure indicate a process not entirely lacking in natural elements.

This case may be compared with the correction of humpbacks due to Pott's disease such as observed by Dr Goret in 1921, which disappeared painlessly in less than four days, and the correction of Antoun Rouhana's ankylosis of the foot (Chapter III).

The progressive cure of John Kelly's clubfoot and *genu valgum* over a period of six years suggests a physiological evolution: but such things are unknown, and human medicine can only obtain results—often all too inadequate—by means of bloody operations, plaster casts and surgical boots.

Diapsychological and parapsychological action on God's part seem to go hand in hand to produce such cures as these. We shall return to them presently.

In point of fact, as we have said, our classifications are only aids to research, facilitating a true analysis of the facts; but God's activity is synthetic and infinitely complex. Thus in Señorita Rebelo's cure the reabsorption of tissue compressing the marrow or the healing of its internal lesions (whichever diagnosis is adopted), the closing of the dorsal fistula and the wounds in the back, the disappearance of urinary and general infection can all be attributed to diapsychological action. But the fact that the first urine passed after the cure was clear implies the disappearance of a certain quantity of pus which must have been lying in the bladder before it. In view of the thickness of this pus it was impossible that none remained in the bladder, and since the last wash-out had been carried out that morning, more must have formed in the meantime. As for the dorsal fistula, it must have been healed from the base outward, thus pushing out the gauze put in by the nurse. But this gauze, as well as the dressing, was found to be quite clean—even if it is admitted that the process of healing began as soon as the dressing was put on, it could not be supposed that the syringing of the fistula was sufficient to clear it completely of its abundant secretion of thick greenish pus. There is here such a perfect harmony of all the factors in the cures as to lead us to assume a combination of diapsychological and parapsychological processes.

We have already pointed out in Chapter II, while dealing with the peculiarities of miraculous cures, that general discomfort and pain, indicating a sort of " crisis " or organic upheaval, is often experienced at the moment when the cure is worked. This is a strong argument in favour of physiological or physical phenomena being produced by divine intervention. But why some cases should be entirely free from it, why some have merely a brief and fleeting sensation and others suffer a really severe attack of pain, we have no idea. Let us take a few examples at randum:

M. Vion-Dury was totally blind for seven years owing to detachment of the retina of both eyes. On August 1st, 1884, he dipped his finger in a little Lourdes water given him by the sister at the hospice of Confort, where he was in hospital, and rubbed his eyes with it. At the third application he felt a violent pain, "as though" he said, "somebody had stuck a knife into my eyes." He thought the sister had given him ammonia by mistake, but at that moment his sight was completely restored.[19] This case was the subject of a report given by Dr Dors of Lyons, who had treated him, to the Paris Congress of Ophthalmology in 1893.

Mlle Delot, suffering from cancer of the pylorus, verified by operation and inoperable, was put into the bath at Lourdes on July 31st, 1926. Terrible pain ensued, together with sensations of burning and oppression in stomach and liver, which spread to the whole abdomen. As she came out of the water this gave way to a wonderful feeling of well-being, vigour and appetite. She was cured.[20]

Mme Augault, suffering from fibroma as already described, was bathed in the morning of August 21st, 1926. She felt as though she were being immersed in boiling oil, and this only ceased on her return to hospital. During the Procession in the afternoon the pain returned: "I felt as though my insides were being torn out." As the Blessed Sacrament passed by the pain left her; she was certain of being cured, and was able to walk.[21]

Mme Pierson, suffering from convulsions of the limbs and trembling as a result of encephalitis, took a partial bath in the piscine on September 12th, 1932. She experienced a violent pain, as though her right arm were being wrenched off. Immediately afterward she was able to move her arm and hand quite easily, and by the next day her recovery was complete.[22]

Mlle Maria de Raedt, gravely ill for several years with acute pyelonephritis coupled with cystitis, on May 30th, 1933, the day before her departure from Lourdes, felt a tearing sensation in the lower abdomen, accompanied by excruciating pain . . . and her disease disappeared.[23]

Similar spasms of pain are to be encountered in the cure of pulmonary tuberculosis, Pott's disease, peritonitis, meningitis, etc. It is by no means rare. But in contrast there are many cures where there is no pain at all, and this suggests that the divine intervention may operate along different lines.

The two cases observed at Knock are particularly enlightening in this respect.

We are, of course, familiar with "the part played by muscular action in the orientation of the trabecular network" and with the fact that "pathology affords daily examples of that capacity for improvisation whereby the framework of fractured bones, fixed in unnatural positions, or of bones joined together by ankylosis, is modified and adapted to meet the needs of the organism. In both cases the cells capable of producing bone structure react under the influence of mechanical action and produce new formations orientated along the lines of the stratigraphy."

The convulsive and painful nature of the attack sustained by John O'Grady when his legs were straightened directs our thoughts toward an accelerated process of bone manipulation, in which the muscular contractions, apparently unco-ordinated, would have their part to play. On the other hand, in the case of John Kelly, whose cure took place painlessly over a period of six years, the first phase made it possible for him to walk, and this allowed muscular activity to intervene in the manipulation of bone and tissue culminating in the perfect cure of the *genu valgum* and clubfoot.

There seems no reason to question the divine action in this case, because the practically instantaneous restoration of rachitic deformities of the bone is quite unknown, and it is common knowledge how many failures are recorded by orthopaedic surgery (which was not used in this instance) in cases like that of John Kelly. Yet this divine action did not follow the same lines in two fairly similar diseases.

In contrast, there was no pain in the case of Peter de Rudder, of which we have just spoken, and the cure was instantaneous ... and the formation of callus, independent of muscular action, was a separate block, not an organically trabecular bone. That greatly strengthens the very tentative hypothesis put forward in his regard.

The variety of methods used in these cures seems to be the sign manual of Him Who is Master of all nature, and Who can work *contra naturam*, *supra naturam* and *praeter naturam* as He sees fit.

Those who observe, comment or describe miraculous cures have too often allowed themselves to be led astray by the word *instantaneousness* which is taken to be an essential condition of a miracle. All too frequently they overlook the fact that theologians understand the term

N

in a relative as well as an absolute sense. What is essential is that the time factor renders it absolutely impossible for the cure to be effected by natural means.

To dispel all doubt in this respect it will suffice to quote two passages from the official *Acts* of the Beatification of Emilie de Rodat, promulgated on March 17th, 1940, and printed in the *Osservatore Romano* the following day. Maria Verdier, suffering from a tumour of the breast which had spread to the ganglions of the armpit, was given up as hopeless by the doctors. In 1894, together with her parents and the Sisters of the Holy Family, she asked God to cure her through the intercession of the Venerable Emilie. We are told that "a relic of the Venerable Emilie was placed over the diseased area. To the astonishment of her own and other doctors Maria was perfectly cured *in the space of a few days*, and from then onward showed no further signs of the disease. Her own two doctors and the experts appointed by the Holy See acknowledged this cure as miraculous." And the Holy Father concluded that "the *instantaneous* and complete cure of Maria Verdier" had been the work of God.

Sister Marie-Thérèse Lesage (Chapter V) is described as having in the evening of June 24th, 1934, recovered "the power of speaking aloud, and shown herself full of energy. Two days later she felt herself completely cured."

Francis Pascal (Chapter VII) reacted violently when placed in the bath—something undoubtedly happened then. Two days later he was bathed without incident and it was only as he was returning across the Rosary Square that he seemed able to see and pointed out a tricycle to his mother. It was not until his return home that he regained the use of his limbs. The cure was therefore not instantaneous in time; but it was relatively instantaneous in comparison with the minimum time required for a natural recovery, even on the assumption that the disease was not incurable.

On October 8th, 1931, Mlle Jaine, suffering from suppurating osteitis of the left wrist, on her third bath in the piscine felt a sharp pain in her knees and left wrist. In the morning of October 10th the dressing was still stained with pus, but by three o'clock in the afternoon both fistulae were closed.[24]

Mlle Bonvalot had two cervical ganglionic fistulae. One was cured on August 23rd, 1931, between eleven and one o'clock, when fresh dressings were put on. The other closed up during the return journey to Lille.[25]

Mlle Invernizzi, with subcutaneous and intramuscular actinomycosis, had nearly a dozen abscesses discharging pus on August 7th, 1931. After the bath several had dried up. On the 8th only three showed signs of slight suppuration. On her return home it was all over.[26]

Finally let us quote the case of M. Clément, reported by Dr Pineau. A malignant cancer of the face, which had spread to the upper lip and lower eyelid, disappeared during sleep in 1912, after a novena to Our Lady of Lourdes, leaving only a swelling the size of a nut in the thickness of the upper lip, and even this disappeared during the day.[27]

These almost instantaneous cures, in which the time factor is only present to an insignificant degree, set a problem as to how far diapsychological and parapsychological action have co-operated in their realisation.

It is undoubtedly in these not quite instantaneous cures that Carrel hoped to find a clue to the processes of cicatrisation. Indeed he had the privilege, as he told Dr Jeanne Bon, of seeing wounds gradually closing before his very eyes. But in spite of this restricted use of the time factor, he wrote on December 13th, 1926: "Some of the facts observed at Lourdes cannot be accounted for by any of the known laws governing the healing of wounds and restoration of tissue. In the course of a miraculous cure the regeneration of the tissues takes place in a manner far in excess of anything observed in the healing of wounds in optimum conditions."[28]

Hence these cures, even those worked over a period, derive from a special sort of physiology, "the physiology of the supernatural," and form a link with those which take place gradually and secretly, and which do not bear the hallmark of the supernatural influence to which they may be due.[29]

We have remarked that Francis Pascal began to see in Lourdes and to walk on his return home. Whether this was a progressive cure of a diapsychological character or really a cure in two stages—either in two supernatural stages or one supernatural stage and one physiological—it is hard to say. But we find among the Fatima cures one which seems typical.

Dr Mendes de Carvalho, who for many years was one of the doctors in charge of the patient, Señora Margarida Texeira Lopes, published a long account of it in the *Voz de Fátima* of January 13th, 1929.

It does not contain the wealth of medical detail we might have desired, for the author has deliberately brought his report within the understanding of the general public, but we do know that several doctors were called in for consultation, that the patient was X-rayed, subjected to numerous laboratory tests and treated with a number of vaccines, particularly autogenous vaccines. The case was therefore complicated, well studied and well treated.

Señora Lopes had suffered for about eight years from a chronic infection which gave rise to multiple and repeated abscesses—several hundred, according to Dr de Carvalho—and her general condition had sunk to a very low ebb.

On October 12th, 1928, she was taken by car to Fatima accompanied by Dr de Carvalho. At that time she had five fully formed abscesses, one in the region of the right elbow and another near the left knee, both open and in full suppuration, the latter obliging her to keep her leg bent. The three other abscesses, gathered but not yet open, were situated on the back of the right shoulder, and made the journey a veritable torture. In addition, dozens of nodules here and there showed where new abscesses were in process of formation.

On the morning of the 13th, after Holy Communion, the patient was taken to the medical bureau where her case was described by Dr de Carvalho and then discussed by the doctors. Meanwhile, she was taken to the sanctuary. As the Bishop of Leiria approached with the Monstrance, she lost consciousness and only came to her senses when the bishop had already blessed several other sick people after her. She was convinced that the Blessed Virgin had granted her a cure.

She noticed that the gauze and cotton wool had fallen off the abscess on her right arm and feared that the pus would soil her clothing. She made an effort to replace the dressing and in so doing discovered that the abscess was healed and that there was no pus. The other abscesses were in a state of marked decline and no longer impeded her movements. The nodules caused by incipient abscesses had disappeared and the areas of skin which had hitherto been hard were now soft and smooth. The sick woman prayed to Our Lady to cure her completely, even at the price of intense suffering.

Señora Lopes returned to her car leaning on her husband's arm. Next day, on her return journey, she visited the monument of Batalha, and arrived home tired but cheerful and lively, with no sign of the numerous nodules, swellings and abscesses, with the exception of those on the right shoulder, now fast disappearing.

She then went through four or five terrible days of high fever, profuse sweating, delirium, violent and extremely painful vomiting, and inability to swallow the slightest nourishment. Then she recovered. The three shoulder abscesses dried up and from that moment not a single nodule has appeared. Gradual realimentation became possible and she completely regained her health.

This case raises a number of interesting points.

There was an initial phase, the instantaneous cure (by parapsychological action?) of an abscess in full suppuration, of several incipient abscesses and of the cutaneous traces of former abscesses. However, there still remained four open abscesses, but in decline. The patient was re-invigorated (by diapsychological action?).

In the second phase an acute attack developed, something like a vaccinal reaction. This cannot be explained by the re-absorption of septic matter from the open or incipient abscesses which disappeared in the first stage, for the fever only began forty-eight hours after their disappearance. Yet the improvement obtained in the first stage made it possible for the patient to walk about at Fatima and Batalha as well as on her arrival home, so producing a definite massage of the remaining abscesses. That a sort of "toxico-microbic" injection was set up in the organism, which then reacted under the dynamic impulse of the first phase and finally emerged victorious, is not a biologically untenable hypothesis.

The occurrence might have been a matter of sheer providence, or of pure chance. But these hardly appeal to the intelligence. In any case it was during the second period that the abscesses closed and the process of infection which had persisted for so many years was finally arrested. A spontaneous or providential biological crisis completed a cure begun, it seems, miraculously.

This leads us naturally to the subject of functional cures where there is no anatomical alteration. Sometimes these are instantaneous or nearly so, and at others occur without any anatomical change at all, or are spread over a period of time.

The cure of Mme Biré of St Gemme de Plaine in Vendée is a case in point.[30] Her health had deteriorated between 1904 and 1906, and on February 11th, 1907, she suddenly developed symptoms of acute meningitis, which later produced a coma lasting for five days. When she recovered consciousness, on February 25th, she was blind, with absence of the light reflexes and double optic atrophy. In August, although almost moribund, she had herself brought to Lourdes. On August 5th, without having been bathed, she regained her sight and health as a priest carrying the Blessed Sacrament passed close by her. She was examined at the medical bureau and Dr Lainey reported: "*Right eye:* pearly-white fundus, central vessels almost imperceptible; otherwise the back of the eye is normal. *Left eye:* pearly-white fundus, central vessels much reduced but about twice the size of those of the right eye; nevertheless they are scarcely one-third of normal. Mme Biré is suffering from optic atrophy of central origin. This is a very serious condition and is recognised by all the authors as incurable." Yet Mme Biré could read the smallest print in a newspaper and her distance vision was perfect.

On September 18th, 1908, Mme Biré was examined in Poitiers by Drs Lainey, Rubbrecht and Creuzé. Dr Rubbrecht wrote to Dr Boissarie: "I have found no trace of the atrophy of the optic nerve described by Dr Lainey. The fundus of both eyes is of a fine rose colour and the vessels are of the normal size. The pupil reacts well to light and to accommodation. In a word, everything is normal."

This case may be compared with that of Gérard Baillie (Chapter VIII) who for nearly two years could see with eyes that should not have seen, and who after two years finally presented a regeneration of the optic nerve.

What happened? There are several possible explanations. Perhaps there remained in the optic nerve (and in the retina in the case of Gérard Baillie) certain tissues not entirely destroyed, not sufficient to ensure vision, but capable of activation by diapsychological or parapsychological supernatural intervention, the anatomical cure following later. Or perhaps we may recall what has been said elsewhere[31] about the conductibility of the nervous fibres of the embryo before myelinisation: "This reminds us that every cell has in itself every aptitude in an elementary form, and that cellular specification in relation to these aptitudes is achieved when the organism reaches a certain degree of complexity. But the process is one of specification, not the development of new aptitudes." In this hypothesis the atrophied tissues, doubtless under the influence of a diapsychological vitalising action, would acquire the power to supply the differentiated elements which would then reproduce themselves.

The case of Mlle Clauzel (Chapter VII) and that of young Daniel Kylmetis (Chapter IX) could be explained along these lines—a functional cure despite the continuance of bone lesions causing compression of the nerves.

A comparable case is that of Mme Pillot, cured at Nancy on February 4th, 1933, during a novena to Our Lady of Lourdes, of functional disorders occasioned by a cerebral tumour for which two craniotomies to relieve the pressure on the brain had been attempted without success. In July 1934 the radiographs of the skull were identical with those before the cure.

This reduction of the miraculous to the sole essential factor introduces us to a third hypothesis. Is it possible that in the cases under consideration the divine intervention, whether diapsychological or parapsychological, is limited to a minimum anatomical or histological modification which permits the restoration of the function but cannot be detected by the means of investigation at our disposal? Thus, speaking of optic atrophy, Hartmann writes: "It is surprising occasionally to find a perfectly white papilla associated with fairly good vision, and sometimes even with normal vision." The appearance of the papilla is therefore not incompatible with a restoration sufficient to ensure vision. On the other hand, although Dr Mollaret's report on young Kylmetis has it that "on the whole the destruction of bone tissue remains," he remarks that "the abscess which was perceptible has now disappeared or diminished to such an extent as to be no longer discernible." The anatomical lesions did not therefore remain in their entirety. The same may be presumed in the case of Mlle Clauzel. The miraculous element seems restricted to a minimum, and these cases would thus form a link with those cures in which there are none of the sudden and obvious changes which betray the divine action to which they are due.

However that may be, whether these functional cures show an economy of the miraculous, divine intervention being limited to the minimum required to restore health, or whether they correspond with the divine will to leave a hallmark of the disease, we begin to trespass here on the theological field, in which we are not competent.

But from the scientific point of view the dissociation of function and lesion gives much food for thought, and may be compared with more or less analogous facts met with in normal medicine. For example, the recovery of all vertebral movement by Mlle Clauzel despite the continued presence of the "parrot beaks" seems to show that it is not the anatomical existence of the latter which is responsible for impotence in similar cases, but rather the pain and reflex contractions caused by the process of inflammation around the osteophytes.

That brings to mind the effects of novocain injections, especially in cases of arthritis and vertebral periarthritis. But no novocain was used here. It reminds one of the spectacular cures worked by ACTH (adrenocorticotropic hormone) or of cortisone. But these hormones were not employed. And if it is suggested that a psychological shock could produce such an effect spontaneously, we reply that it would still not occur instantaneously. Moreover, the patient had suffered the shock of a pilgrimage to Lourdes without success, and since she had long been resigned to her fate, prayed for other intentions than her own recovery, and assisted at Holy Mass in the very ordinary village church, there is nothing on which to base any special psychological shock.

Could diapsychological action have stimulated an intense production of the appropriate hormones and thus bring about a miraculous cure? It is a possible explanation.

Thus miraculous cures take their place between the action of God on the soul, vital principle of the human creature, on the one hand, and the action of God the Creator on the very essence of the matter constituting the human body on the other, the while God in His power combines and regulates these actions as He pleases.

We have shown (in Chapter II) how the Church demands that there should be no relapse for a considerable time before recognising a cure as miraculous. The Lourdes Medical Bureau makes no pronouncement until the cure has been maintained for a year.

But what if there is a relapse or recurrence after the year is over, or after the period considered sufficient by the ecclesiastical authorities?

That in no way disproves God's intervention. A miraculous cure is not a guarantee of longevity nor of immunity from future disease. The miraculous cure consists in the disappearance of the actual morbid condition in circumstances which rule out any spontaneous development capable of producing such an effect naturally, and point to the likelihood of divine intervention. There is no reason to suppose that the person cured should enjoy the permanent miracle of freedom from other diseases or even from that from which he was cured.

When a tuberculous patient recovers in the ordinary way from Pott's disease, nobody denies the cure, even though he may suffer a further pulmonary or glandular attack. His Pott's disease is cured, but his tendency to tuberculosis remains. Disease does not imply the mere presence of germs in the organism: it implies that the organism is being defeated in its warfare with those germs. Even a recurrence of the Pott's disease does not give grounds for denying that there was a temporary recovery.

When a cardiac patient recovers from an attack and is able to resume his daily life, it cannot be denied that his return to health (although he is still potentially a cardiac case) was due to the digitalis or ouabaïn with which he was treated. Nor does a recurrence in any way belie the previous recovery. In the same way when acute articular rheumatism is arrested by the use of salicylates, a further relapse disproves neither the original cure nor the efficacy of the treatment.

In addition it is quite unreasonable and unscientific to question a cure like that of Mme Rouchel in 1903, as some have done, because of a relapse five years later. This lady had suffered for nine years from lupus which had attacked a great part of her face and pierced the cheek and soft palate. She was instantaneously delivered from her affliction, with the exception of a small area on the upper lip, loss of substance being made good, and remained cured until 1908, when the disease reappeared. But neither the continuance of a small local lesion nor the relapse after five years prevent there having been an instantaneous cure of considerable lesions. "It is beyond question," writes Dr Le Bec, "that the disease disappeared by a process exceeding the powers of nature. . . . The reality of this cicatrisation was not denied by any of the doctors opposed to Lourdes who examined the patient at Metz. Dr Boissarie was therefore perfectly right in saying that such cicatrisation cannot be explained by natural means. . . . It was therefore a miracle."[32]

One of us has for nearly forty years been personally acquainted with Mlle Marie Briffaut, cured instantaneously in 1893 of suppurating osteitis with necrosis of the head of the femur and elimination of sequestra. In 1912 she was in perfect health except for some recent dyspeptic trouble. Several years later she developed chronic tubercular nephritis. It is clear that this new tuberculous infection in no way undermines the apparently miraculous character of the cure of the osteitis thirty years previously.

Nevertheless if we remember that in the case of Mme Hébert, cured of pulmonary tuberculosis in 1900, the skin reaction had latterly been found to be negative, we are led to suspect differences of degree between apparently identical cures, differences which only our modern means of biological investigation or the further progress of the person's health enable us to judge.

Nor should the cures in which a relapse or recurrence takes place before the time fixed by ecclesiastical authority or medical organisations be overlooked. A relapse occurring shortly after the cure is disturbing, but does nothing to destroy the fact of an objectively established cure. Far from short-circuiting the problem of an extraordinary cure, it is an added complication. The scientific problem remains: and Huysmans has shown what questions are raised from the metaphysical point of view by the cure of a child of osteitis with abscesses, which did not last.[33] Case histories of this sort should be carefully compiled and studied.

We have observed elsewhere that supernatural favours are independent of the psychology of the individual. When St Francis of Assisi received the stigmata he was not thinking of Christ's wounds but of the meaning of his vision of the crucified seraph. Levitation, luminosity and other similar phenomena are often produced without their subject being conscious of them. In miraculous cures the same gratuitous character of the favour granted and the absence of psychological co-operation on the part of the recipient are often fully evident.

This is put beyond any shadow of doubt by the cures of children of which several instances have been given in these pages. M. Gargam, cured in 1899 of paraplegia resulting from a railway accident, had no faith, and refused to pray when his mother brought him to Lourdes. As for M. Clément, his cancer was cured, as we have said, during sleep, and Dr Pineau made it clear that the novena to Our Lady of Lourdes had been made *by his two daughters*. Mlle Fretel did not realise that she was at Lourdes until after she had received a particle of the Sacred Host, and by then her cure had already begun. Then there are many who were cured after having accepted their affliction and prayed, like Mlle Clauzel, for quite different intentions, their family, their country, a conversion, and not for their own recovery at all.

This lack of psychological co-operation clearly does away with the theory of auto-suggestion, which is often put forward on the flimsiest grounds, and supports that of an influence independent of the subject.

The sick who are cured miraculously (as far as we can judge) are frequently chronic, incurable invalids, who have had to be given morphine, sometimes in considerable doses.

As early as 1890 Dr Boissarie recorded a case of morphinomania of two years' duration (in which as much as $7\frac{1}{2}$-9 grains were taken in a day) which was broken off suddenly, although the lesion and the pain which had occasioned it still remained.

Among the cases quoted in these pages, it will be noted that Mlle Fretel felt no further need of morphine after her cure, whereas it took Mme Martin six months to free herself from her craving.

We can do no more than mention these differences of behaviour, but although they are of secondary importance, they would repay close examination both from the physiological and psychological points of view.

The study of miraculous cures cannot afford to overlook the subsidiary effects or by-products which they entail. Since they exist, they cannot be left out of account, and if their explanation has any bearing on our discussion, they cannot be dismissed as of no interest.

One of these is particularly noteworthy. It is the interior conviction of having been cured, experienced in certain cases, whereby the sick person, without making the slightest movement, *knows* within himself that he is cured, that he can get up, walk, eat, work. Mlle Fretel felt as though hands were raising her up or taking hold of hers, so that she looked round to see who was helping her. Mme Rouchet's dressing came undone twice in spite of her efforts to fasten it, so that she had to return to the hospital to have it put on properly, and the cure was discovered. Señora Lopes' dressings fell off of their own accord, and she was thus able to see that the abscesses were closed. We are personally acquainted with a case in which a holy nun, having received a telegram that a sick woman was desperately ill, wired back that she was cured . . . and so she was.

A careful study of the case histories would in all probability reveal many such facts, which might be prudently called "metapsychological," but which only a superficial mind would refuse to consider.

The various peculiarities of miraculous or presumably miraculous cures touched upon in this chapter show how complex is their study. Some doctors might prefer us to describe only such cases as that of Francis Pascal because they feel the others to be less conclusive.

We believe that this method would have been utterly unscientific and wrong. Our object in this work is not to prove the existence of miracles. That has been done by experience since the time of Moses and the burning bush, Ezechias and the shadow on the wall, and St Thomas and the Saviour's wounds, to say nothing of the philosophical proofs. Our intention has been to study miraculous or presumably miraculous cures worked in our own day which have passed the test of our modern scientific knowledge. To pick and choose would have meant falsifying the whole question. On the contrary, we had to give as wide a selection as possible, ranging from obvious (and officially recognised) cures to merely probable or possible ones. In present-day medicine the mixed and atypical forms of diseases are not the least interesting and instructive. Very often these very forms are not the least authentic aspects of the affection under consideration.

For the reasons we have outlined, God's intervention may be more or less striking, more or less far-reaching, more or less mingled with natural, secondary or supplementary elements. It is not for us to demand of God that His action conform to any given pattern. Our rôle and duty as men and as scientists is to try to recognise that action, under whatever guise it may be found.

With this in view it is right and proper to record those cures which we suspect of being miraculous as they take place, even if certain essential documents are not available. Comparison with other cases and certain of their secondary or non-medical details may throw light upon or provide confirmation of our researches. That means that those who draw up reports on these cases should not hesitate to include, not merely the exclusively medical details, but also such circumstantial data as the psychological condition of the patient or his family circle, any facts which appear to have a mystical or metapsychological flavour, and the like. Cures presumed to be miraculous overlap the fields of medicine and of mysticism, and we cannot attain to any true knowledge of them without taking account of *all* the elements of their make-up, even if they seem to go far beyond the bounds of medicine. . . . But how could they be said to go beyond the bounds of medicine if they are involved in the development of disease? The doctor has to widen his horizon if he wishes to grasp the total cause of the cure. For that reason the study of presumably miraculous cures must be carried out calmly, without prejudice, without wearing blinkers, without making greater demands than in normal medicine, with one end in view—to know the truth. For the Christian, if the cure is proved to be natural, it is, as St Augustine would say, the natural work of God. If miraculous, then it is an exceptional mark of God's loving care and almighty power.

CONCLUSION

Now that we have arrived at the end of our study, we can see developing before our eyes a synthesis of all the facts examined, of all the data we have been led to consider, and of all the hypotheses suggested by them.

From the first, the whole genesis of the world, revelation, theology, the latest scientific conceptions of matter, the examination of great—we may say classical—miracles, have all helped to show that the study of miracles demands that we raise and broaden our views beyond their present anthropomorphic limits and rise above the level of the sort of law laid down dogmatically by nineteenth-century scientists, which are now quite out of date.

We have seen that miraculous cures are the subject of the most rigorous investigation and examination by doctors, biologists and theologians. They do not form a clearly marked class of facts; rather they resemble a sort of pyramid, those at the base mingling with the host of natural cures, but the higher they rise above that base, the more clearly do certain of their characteristics appear, until finally we arrive at the topmost regions of the pyramid, those of the rare phenomena which far outstrip normal possibility and allow us to catch a far-off glimpse of their almighty Author.

From quite recent events, examined and verified with all the meticulous care and the most accurate techniques possible, it is evident—as had always been realised—that in miraculous cures there is no constant factor, whether of age, sex, nature of the disease, place or treatment. But one thing is always present: there is invariably an appeal to God. As Alexis Carrel says, "Everything happens as though God were listening to Man and answering him."[34]

When we look closer into the intimate nature of miraculous activity, we realise that there is no question of arbitrary, irrational action, upsetting the order of things, but instead, the action of an overwhelming power, which seems to work either directly or by means of the activated vital principle or of biological and physical factors which modern science is only just beginning to discover. Thus, far from leading us to hope that one day we shall find a natural explanation of miraculous cures, the biological and physical factors whose presence we can discern or suspect demand an intelligent Power to set them in motion, the Master and Controller of the very essence of matter.

The study of miraculous cures in the light of modern science opens for us a wonderful field of scientific possibilities, and points the way to God Himself.

o

NOTES

NOTES TO CHAPTER I

1. For the theology of miracles, cf. Cardinal Lépicier, *Le Miracle*, Desclée de Brouwer, 1936.

2. Cf. Lecomte du Nouy, *L'Homme devant la Science*, Paris, 1939; *L'Homme et sa Destinée*, Paris, 1949; Philippe Olmer, *La Structure des Choses*, Paris, 1950.

3. Alexis Carrel, *La Prière*, Paris, 1947, p. 25.

4. Olmer, op. cit., p. 219.

5. M. Poujoulat, *Histoire de Saint Augustin*, Paris, 1852, II, p. 219.

6. Fr Jean Rivière, professor of apologetics in the Catholic theological faculty of the University of Strasbourg, writes in the *Dictionnaire des Connaissances Religieuses*, Paris, 1925 (s.v.): "We must at all costs be careful not to introduce into the notion of 'miracle' any idea which might seem to imply disorder, like those formulae made fashionable by the apologists of the eighteenth century: *'violation of the laws of nature,' 'fact contrary to natural laws.'* As definitions they were unwise and apt to compromise miracles in the judgment of right reason under the pretext of emphasising their divine character. . . . A miracle may be defined as an event, the extra-ordinary appearance and religious character of which indicates a special intervention of God in nature with a spiritual end in view."

7. Cf. IV Kings 5, Jonas 2. Whether the story of Jonas be fact or parable, the discovery of the whale-shark (rhineodon typus), which is capable of swallowing a 200 lb. fish whole, undermines the old argument against its historicity. Cf. Young, *Les Requins*, Paris, 1934.

8. Lépicier, op. cit., p. 518.

9. Exodus, 7 and 8.

10. Matthew, 24, 24. (All quotations are from Mgr Knox's translation. *Tr.*)

11. Josue, 10, 13.

12. Académie des Sciences, May 3rd, 1943.

13. Josue, 10, 11. (Both the Douay and Knox versions refer to "hailstones." *Tr.*)

14. IV Kings, 20, 8-11.

15. On October 7th, 1571, about five o'clock in the afternoon, the Pope was in conference with a number of prelates when he suddenly rose, went to the window, opened it, and stood there in profound contemplation for several minutes. Then he turned, deeply moved, and ordered prayers of thanksgiving to be said for the victory which had just been won. It was not until several days later that official news of the battle of Lepanto was received at the Vatican.

16. It is well known that a mirage at sea, by reflection or refraction in the upper strata of the atmosphere, can make visible objects hundreds of miles away.

17. Cf. Barthas et Fonseca, *Fatima*, Toulouse, 1942.

18. Exodus, 14, 21-22.

19. Josue, 3, 14-17.

20. Exodus 7, 20-21.

21. John, 2, 3-10.

22. A short account of this little known saint will be found in Butler, *Lives of the Saints*, ed. Thurston, May volume, p. 168. (Tr.)

23. Cf. Olivier Leroy, "De la Multiplication miraculeuse des Biens," in *La Vie Spirituelle*, March and April, 1937.

24. In the prodigies attributed to Al-Allaj, martyr-mystic of Islam, it would appear that multiplication of substance is not involved, but rather a transfer: a bowl of sweetmeats was found to have come from a confectioner's shop whence it had disappeared. Cf. Massignon, *Al-Allaj, martyr mystique de l'Islam*, Paris, 1922; Leroy, op. cit.

25. Exodus, 10, 12-19.

26. Genesis, 30, 31-43.
27. On Acts 9, 1-22.
28. Cf. Monin, *Notre-Dame de Beauraing*, Desclée de Brouwer, 1949.
29. Landouzy was a famous French doctor and teacher of medical subjects. (Tr.)
30. Leo XIII.
31. Olmer, op. cit., p. 79.
32. This is no more than an interesting scientific hypothesis in no way endorsed by theological opinion. (Tr.)
33. Cf. Bon, *Précis de Médecine catholique*, Paris, 1936, p. 295.
34. Lépicier, op. cit., p. 13.
35. Cf. Bon, *La Mort et ses Problèmes*, Paris, 1948, chapter I.
36. Daniel 3.
37. Cf. Bon, op. cit., p. 247.
38. Daniel 3, 49-50.
39. Ibid. 47-48.
40. Cardinal Lépicier shows that the division of the waters of the Red Sea before the Hebrews may be assigned to the first or third category according as we suppose God's intervention to have been direct or by means of an angel. These classifications have no absolute value, but are relative to our assumptions regarding God's way of acting.

NOTES TO CHAPTER II

1. Wisdom 1, 13-15.
2. Cf. Le Bec, *Les Preuves médicales du Miracle*, Paris 1921.
3. We have long been familiar with the toxic accidents involved in the re-absorption of tumours under treat-ment by radio-therapy. Quite recently Professor Laffont of Algiers attributed the fatal accidents occurring in cases of cancer treated with thyroxin to the lysis of the tumours. Moreover, Dr Monnet of Lyons concludes that the cardiac collapse of a typhoid patient after a

large dose of chloromycetin was due to the sudden liberation of endotoxin through lysis of the microbes.

4. Cf. *Société médicale des Hôpitaux de Paris*, October 27th, 1950. (This refers to continental liberalism, condemned by Pope Pius IX in the *Syllabus* of 1864. Tr.)

5. Cf. *Annales des Sciences psychiques*, 1907.

6. M. Gaud, *De certains processus psychiques de guérison*, Lyon, 1907; Mme Jeanne Bon, *Thèse sur quelques guérisons de Lourdes*, Lyons, 1912; Do Souto, *Lourdes e a Medicina*, Coimbra, 1923; H. Monnier, *Etude médicale de quelques guérisons survenues à Lourdes*, Paris, 1930; A. Guarner, *De l'instantanéité des guérisons de Lourdes*, Algiers, 1939; J. Guérin, *Quelques réflexions médicales sur les guérisons de Lourdes*, Bordeaux, 1939; R. Ferron, *Etude sur les guérisons dites miraculeuses*, Paris, 1939; N. Mittler, *Des guérisons dites "miraculeuses" aux guérisseurs et à leurs clients*, Paris, 1940.

7. Mark, 1, 45.

8. Thus there exists in Ceylon, at Pandateruppu, a church built in 1945 in honour of Our Lady of Fatima. The local people have begun to call it Putumai Kovil, "The church of the miracles." But Father Gesland, its founder and rector, has told us that he is often the last to hear of these miracles. The sick are cured and simply return home. Similarly William Coyne, the historian of Knock, writes: "One of the most impressive of the recent cures comes from Limerick. Two children suffering from tuberculous ganglions were cured instantaneously on July 11th, 1937, while visiting the shrine. The mother said nothing for about four years because of the commonly accepted idea that it would not be right to speak of such a favour." (Cf. *Cnoc Mhuire*, p. 181.) Pierre Bouriette (chap. VI) was an exception.

9. The *Bulletin de l'Association médicale internationale de Notre-Dame de Lourdes*, which has published medical reports on the cures at Lourdes since 1928, would welcome similar reports of miraculous cures wherever they may be worked. The *Bulletin* will be quoted in these pages as *Bulletin A.M.I.L.*

NOTES TO CHAPTER III

1. Cf. Van der Elst, *Vraies et fausses guérisons miraculeuses*, Paris, 1924.

2. Cf. *Brilhante Milagre em Fatima*, Uniao grafica, Lisbon, 1945.

3. The bureau in 1951 comprised twelve doctors. The secretary is Dr George Maguire, Claremorris. He writes: "The bureau have investigated a number of claims, but so far have not expressed the opinion that any of the cures can be looked on as miraculous." This should be borne in mind in regard to what follows. (Tr.)

4. Published by O'Gorman, Galway, 5th impression, 1949.

5. Rickets is now generally curable by vitamin D. The non-curability here refers to the bony deformities. These, however, are now (1955) sometimes curable by ortho-paedic measures—a possibility not then envisaged, perhaps, but now possible due to recent advances in many branches of medical science. (Tr.)

6. Coyne, op. cit., p. 167.

7. Coyne, op. cit., p. 174.

8. Account written by Mother M. Immacolata Natale, Collegio femminile Archangelo Raffaele, Acireale, in the bulletin, *Il Rosario e la nuova Pompeii*, 1941.

9. Ibid., 1949.

10. It is perhaps open to doubt whether all the requirements of a miraculous cure, particularly that of rapidity, are present in this case. (Tr.)

11. Cf. Gorel, *La Sainte Maison de Lorette*, Paris, 1936; J. S. Northcote, *Celebrated Sanctuaries of the Madonna*, London, 1868; Aradi, *Shrines to Our Lady Around the World*, New York, 1954. (The present statue is a copy of the ancient original, destroyed by fire in 1921. Tr.)

12. Cf. H. P. Bergeron, *Le Frère André*, Montreal, 1947.

13. Cf. V. Hulselmans, *Padre Eustaquio*, Rio de Janeiro, 1944; Mouly, *Des Miracles révolutionnent l'Amérique*, Paris, 1946.

14. Cf. Nasri Rizcallah, *Charbel Makhlouf*, Paris, 1950.

NOTES TO CHAPTER IV

1. This chapter was written by Canon Gardié, theologian of the Archdiocese of Bordeaux, to whose kindness and learning we owe our gratitude.
2. The following section is derived almost entirely from the Code of Canon Law, canons 1999-2141, which deal with this procedure. We have thought it wiser not to encumber the text with unnecessary references to the individual canons. (Tr.)
3. Blessed Claude was beatified on June 16th, 1929. (Tr.)
4. Similarly the general congregation met and discussed the cause of Saint Pius X on January 30th, 1951, and the decree was published on February 11th. (Tr.)

NOTES TO CHAPTER V

1. It may be remarked that the following cases are described summarily, without the relevant medical details and certificates. The full procedure described in the foregoing chapter has, however, been carried out in all its rigour in each instance. (Tr.)
2. The disease is now sometimes curable by streptomycin, which was not then available. (Tr.)
3. It is interesting to notice in passing that her father had died of cancer of the lips.

NOTES TO CHAPTER VI

1. The bureau was started unofficially in 1882.
2. Alexis Carrel acted thus in 1903, when faced with Marie Bailly's recovery from tuberculous peritonitis, which occurred in his presence and which he recorded. It was not until years later that he drew the logical conclusion from his observations. Cf. *Voyage to Lourdes*, Harper, New York.
3. This sort of phenomenon is not uncommon at Lourdes— one clearly outside the laws of nature.

4. Alexis Carrel has drawn attention to the fact that the only constant relationship between cure and any other activity is that between cure and prayer. (Tr.)

5. Dr Vallet, now retired to Paimpol, still comes to Lourdes annually as a pilgrim and the bureau is fortunate in having his experience and advice to call upon.

6. As of 1950.

7. These included fifty-seven fractures in 1949.

8. The Lourdes Hospitalité is the lay and ecclesiastical body administering the grotto. It has branches in many dioceses which help to run the pilgrimages.

9. Pharmacists and others with suitable qualifications also register here, but are not as a rule allowed to attend clinical sessions.

10. Dr Aumont's place was taken in 1951 by Dr Joseph Pellissier, an experienced psychiatrist from Marseilles, who continues to carry out the X-ray photography as well.

11. Others deserving thanks include Professors Dirken, de Gromingen and Dikstra; M. le Comte de Beauchamp (who was responsible for the original suggestion); the French Red Cross, particularly M. Dasset, its secretary, Colonel Bouvier, its president, and M. Mammet, hospitaller of Lourdes. Owing to their efforts the apparatus was brought into France free of duty. While others would prefer not to be named, the writers feel that those of our parliamentary friends who put in a good word with the treasury and director of customs will appreciate the gratitude of all medical men connected with Lourdes. In the hands of Dr Pellissier this equipment gives first-class results and the X-ray library is beginning to assume impressive proportions. [1950.]

NOTES TO CHAPTER VII

1. We are indebted to the president of the Aix canonical commission for permission to publish the proceedings of that body.

2. The word here seems to be used symptomatically; it does not seem that gastric aspiration was performed. (Tr.)

3. It is doubtful if all doctors would subscribe to the view that the "parrot beaks" were responsible for symptoms. However, inflammatory processes around these may have contributed to the symptomatology of this case. (Tr.)

4. These improvements may have been due to release of adrenal hormones. (Tr.)

5. Two X-ray pictures are included in the original French text. They do not add materially to the information, but are labelled as follows: (1) Cervical vertebrae in 1945 (after the cure). Osteophytes can be seen projecting from the upper and lower borders of the vertebral bodies. (2) Dorsal spine, 1945. Osteophytes present (though less striking). The space between D8 and D9 (noted on X-ray) is irregularly denser than the others. (Tr.)

6. We are indebted to the president of the Nice diocese canonical commission for permission to examine the documents of that body relevant to this case. We are also indebted to his Lordship the Bishop of Nice for authority to publish the findings.

7. The data concerning the illness of the patient from January 1938 to October 1948 is taken from the detailed report of Dr Alphonse Pellé, professor of the School of Medicine, Rennes.

8. First report of the Bureau of Medical Records.

9. Evidence given by patient to the canonical commission.

NOTES TO CHAPTER VIII

1. The French word *chorio-retinite* has been translated throughout as choroiditis. (Tr.)

2. Among vertebrata natural regeneration of retina and optic nerve has been noted in grafting experiments with salamanders. Cf. reports by L. S. Stone and his collaborators, Zaur, Farthing and Ellison (1930-45).

3. The alternative is that the majority of the doctors involved in the case were mistaken. In view of the facts, this is unlikely. Yet another alternative is that they were concerned in a giant hoax. This also seems difficult to credit. (Tr.)

4. *Neuro-végétatif* in the French has been translated throughout this section simply as 'nervous'. The writer is referring probably to disordered autonomic function suggested by the symptoms of intestinal movement. (Tr.)

NOTES TO CHAPTER X

1. In writing this chapter we have drawn upon the cases described in these pages and the modern cures recorded in the *Bulletin de l'Association médicale internationale de Notre-Dame de Lourdes*. But Dr Boissarie's books, particularly the often reprinted *L'Oeuvre de Lourdes*, although catering to a wide public, contain a valuable documentation that may be consulted with profit in this respect.

2. The absence of a medical document or its faulty compilation may prevent the recognition of a miracle, but it cannot prevent it from having taken place. The Church does not forbid anybody privately to consider himself cured by a miracle, to put up an ex-voto in a sanctuary, or to have a Mass said privately in thanksgiving.

3. Cf. Genesis 1, 26, 28.

4. Some scientists might say that this assurance could never be given. The Church is satisfied with the statement that the "laws of natural science", as currently understood and known, cannot account for the data concerned. No account can be given in natural terms, for example, to explain the sudden disappearance of malignant tissues as in the case of Mme Rose Martin.

5. *Bibliothèque de Médecine catholique*, under the general direction of Dr Henri Bon.

6. Father Jean Riviére, already quoted (Chapter I, Note 6), writes as follows (op. cit): "The nature and circumstances of certain events, such as the sudden healing of

muscular or bone lesions, the instantaneous clearing of deep-seated poisoning, the restoration of long atrophied functions, whatever secondary causes may have intervened, manifest their exceptional and superhuman origin."

7. Cf. Dr Bon's unpublished lecture read to the Société Médicale de Saint-Luc, Marseilles, February 2nd, 1942, on *Les Interventions de Dieu dans la Physiologie humaine.*

8. It may cause some surprise that we should use such restraint in speaking of "abnormal degree," "secondary effect." Mlle Fretel's physical condition, rendered infinitely more serious by the tuberculous infection which had led her to the brink of the grave, was quite different from that of the wretched victims of the German concentration camps, who weighed less than half their usual weight, and failed to survive their liberation by the Allies because they would not submit to a properly regulated course of realimentation and ate anything they could lay their hands on. At that stage of emaciation (we have had in our clinic patients weighing fifty-six lbs. instead of 133!), the basal metabolism is greatly reduced (as much as 30 per cent.). This makes possible a rapid increase in weight by means of liquid nourishment or a regular diet of not more than 3,000 calories, but spells disaster to one who gluts himself with any kind of food. Mlle Fretel seems to have weighed only thirty-one lbs. less than her usual weight, and to make that up in sixteen days is "abnormal." We cannot say for certain that it goes beyond the capacity of nature, but it does indicate that nature has been "dynamised." It is therefore a "secondary effect of an extraordinary activation."

Consequently a more detailed analysis than is commonly made of miraculous cures would reveal a distinction between the essential, primary effects of miraculous action and the secondary effects by which it is known. There are, of course, the more mundane effects of a return to health, but we may leave these to one side. But this distinction between the primary and secondary results seems to us to be of importance because to confuse them would be to dim the transcendence of miraculous action, which is so much more evident when the biological problem is tackled squarely, as we shall see in a moment in the case of Sister Marie-Marguerite.

9. Cf. Professor Lemière in the *Bulletin de la Société Médicale de Saint-Luc*, 1926, p. 90.

10. Bulletin A.M.I.L., 1929, p. 184.

11. Ibid., p. 73.

12. Bulletin A.M.I.L., July 1946, p. 8.

13. The time taken for the feeling of compression to pass down her body.

14. For example, using Carré's simple apparatus.

15. Cf. Bon, *La Mort et ses Problémes*, p. 253.

16. Perhaps this is the place to recall Louis de Broglie's remarks on the fact that at the level of quantum physics only a weak causality survives, which does not prevent "one cause producing one or other of several possible effects, with only a certain probability that one effect will be produced rather than another. . . . If we add that the most important vital phenomena seem to occur within the cells or even the cellular nuclei at the various atomic levels, it will appear that the impossibility of establishing a definite determinism at that level may have a predominant influence on the development of our ideas on everything pertaining to life, and may perhaps bring new light to bear on many of the traditional problems of philosophy." *L'Avenir de la Science*, Paris, 1941.

17. Cf. Bulletin A.M.I.L., 1929, p. 114.

18. We know that an inherent stimulant activity of this kind is attributed to *microsomes*, cytoplasmic corpuscles of the same chemical ribonucleoprotein composition as the protein virus extracted from the higher virous plants and recently discovered by A. Claude. These microsomes, like the viruses, possess the power of autocatalytic growth, and are among the permanent elements of the cytoplasm. They play a fundamental rôle in the synthesis of the specific proteins.

19. Bulletin A.M.I.L., 1933, p. 44.
20. Bulletin A.M.I.L., 1928, p. 20.
21. Bulletin A.M.I.L., 1929, p. 73.
22. Bulletin A.M.I.L., 1934, p. 51.
23. Bulletin A.M.I.L., 1934, p. 114.
24. Bulletin A.M.I.L., 1933, p. 8.
25. Bulletin A.M.I.L., 1931, p. 164.
26. Bulletin A.M.I.L., 1933, p. 40.
27. Bulletin A.M.I.L., 1936, p. 194.
28. Bulletin A.M.I.L., 1931, p. 29.
29. Cf. Kylmetis case.
30. Bulletin A.M.I.L., 1934, p. 123.
31. Bon, "La Personnalité humaine avant la Naissance," in *Bulletin de la Société Médicale de Saint-Luc*, April 1948.
32. "Causes d'Erreurs et Difficultés dans la Reconnaissance des Guérisons miraculeuses," in *Bulletin de la Société Médicale de Saint-Luc*, 1932.
33. Cf. *The Crowds of Lourdes*, tr. Mitchell, London, 1925, pp. 65, 131, 162.
34. *La Prière*, Paris, 1947, p. 25.

APPENDIX 1

In the interval between this translation reaching the publisher and its going to the printers, three papers have appeared in the *British Medical Journal* which are relevant to the subject of miracles in general. It seemed opportune to comment upon them in an appendix.

The first (V. B. Levison, Feb. 19, 1955, p. 458) is concerned with a case—and refers to others—of spontaneous regression of melanotic carcinoma—a form of pigmented cancer. That this can happen is well recognised, and accounts for the scepticism with which some doctors approach the question of miraculous recovery from cancer. However, in none of the cases of which the medical translator has read is there any indication that they were instantaneous in the way that that of Mme Martin was, for instance.

The moral of this fact—i.e. that some cancers can apparently disappear spontaneously—is twofold. First, the fourth of Pope Benedict XIV's conditions for declaring a cure miraculous should be most strictly applied—the cure must be instantaneous. (The other feature distinguishing miraculous cures from non-miraculous ones is the usually complete absence of any convalescence.) Secondly, the believing Catholic, and particularly the layman, must approach the unbelief of the non-Catholic, particularly if the latter be a doctor, with gentleness and respect, remembering that he (the non-Catholic) may well have read of, or actually had experience of, cases of spontaneous regression of a firmly diagnosed cancer.

The second paper (S. K. Karagula and E. S. Robertson, Mar. 26, 1955, p. 748) is concerned with the production of what are called epileptic hallucinations—the seeing of visions, the hearing of voices. For example, the visions of Saint Joan of Arc may well be dismissed as forms of epileptic hallucinations by a psychiatrist. His doubts must be treated with respect. The Catholic apologist must be aware that such phenomena do occur and have a medical, secondary or proximate explanation. To decide their nature, to determine whether they come from God, requires that all the circumstances of the case be taken into account and, most vital, that the history of the individual (his or her story), and the Church's judgment, be carefully considered. However, there is no reason why Almighty God should not produce visions, e.g. of an angel, by acting on the cerebral cortex. Or He might permit an angel to act directly in this way. Neither of these modes of activity would automatically invalidate the vision. He is, after all, Lord of electrons, atoms, molecules, cells and nerve tracts as well as Lord of visible creation. The mechanics of visions, their proximate causes, are relatively unimportant. Their relationship to God and man requires that all the attendant circumstances and history of the particular case be taken into account before any decision is reached.

The believer, then, should go carefully in discussing these questions with his contemporaries, making himself familiar with the technical evidence and opinions before becoming responsible for dogmatic or public pronouncements. This is, after all, the Church's own attitude. It is worth noting how few of the so-called miraculous cures (including some described in this book) have actually been pronounced miraculous by the Church.

Finally, those interested in the problems here discussed should note a short paper (L. Rose, April 12, 1954, p. 1329) that illustrates some of the pitfalls that face those investigating alleged paranormal cures.

APPENDIX 2

A[In the early 1940s both translators met Jack Traynor, at that time an apparently very fit man, who had been gravely wounded at Gallipoli. He was given a 100 per cent. disability pension by the British Government which, despite his apparent complete cure at Lourdes, he was alleged to be entitled to draw till he died. (His death was apparently unconnected with his wounds.)

He was cured of traumatic epilepsy and all the paralytic sequelae of gunshot wounds, which severed one brachial plexus. His cure involved the closure of a large hole in the skull and, it seems, the complete disappearance of pieces of metal embedded in his brain. A popular account of this man's history is published by the Catholic Truth Society, London. It would be interesting to see the Ministry of Pensions' notes on his case.

B[There can be little doubt from the record given in this book of Mlle Clauzel's case that (1) she suffered from a serious illness which apparently involved the nervous system, (2) that this illness appeared, in her medical attendant's opinion, to be about to kill her, and (3) that she was *suddenly* cured on a feast of Our Lady, during Mass. The medical translator feels that, had he sat on the medical bodies concerned with judging the medical documents, while he would have admitted the above, he would have abstained from voting for or against "supernatural intervention" in this case. His reason for so doing would rest on the fact that the diagnosis was not quite clearcut, at least as far as the documents here given are concerned. (It should be made clear to non-Catholic readers that a Catholic is not bound to accept as miraculous any events other than those in the Bible which the Universal Church has declared are miracles. It should be noted too that the Church's notion and definition of "miracle" is very pertinent to this question.)